SEEING GOD IN EACH OTHER

SEEING GOD
IN EACH OTHER

Edited by Sheryl A. Kujawa-Holbrook

MOREHOUSE PUBLISHING

HARRISBURG PENNSYLVANIA

Morehouse Publishing, P.O. Box 1321, Harrisburg, PA 17105

Morehouse Publishing, 455 Fifth Avenue, New York, NY 10016

Morehouse Publishing is an imprint of Church Publishing Incorporated.

Cover design by Wesley Hoke

Library of Congress Cataloging-in-Publication Data

Seeing God in each other / edited by Sheryl A. Kujawa-Holbrook.
    p.   cm.
    Includes bibliographical references (p.   ).
    ISBN 0-8192-2186-4 (pbk.)
    1. Race relations—Religious aspects—Episcopal Church. 2. Episcopal Church—Doctrines. I. Kujawa-Holbrook, Sheryl A.
    BX5979.5.R32S44   2006
    270.089—dc22

                                    2005025133

Printed in the United States of America

06 07 08 09 10   10 9 8 7 6 5 4 3 2 1

CONTENTS

INTRODUCTION

Jayne J. Oasin

As part of our Anglican heritage, we believe in the importance of the doctrine of the Incarnation. The term, from the Latin, literally means "enfleshment." The doctrine of the Incarnation recognizes Jesus as both fully human and fully divine. Thus the theme of the anti-racism program of the Episcopal Church, "Seeing the Face of God in Each Other," springs directly from our denominational heritage. It also serves to ground anti-racism within the tradition of the church, and as an integral component of how we live together as Christians. One of the challenges I encounter again and again as we sponsor anti-racism workshops and programs across the Episcopal Church is that anti-racism is not "spiritual," but rather an exercise in "political correctness." Yet, "Seeing the Face of God in Each Other," while not only part of a lifelong spiritual process, is integral to our vocation as Christians living within a pluralistic world.

As a Christian and as a member of the Episcopal Church, I have asked myself, where do I go for strength and help as I engage anti-racism as a critical ministry of helping to create a vision of the reign of God? A phrase from the Book of Common Prayer sounds in my head like a leitmotif: "Deliver us from the presumption of coming to this table for solace only and not for strength. . . ." And to the table my colleagues in the anti-racism and anti-oppression work are blessed to go again and again to be refreshed and refilled with the Holy Spirit who is both our comforter and guide in this most crucial ministry of the church. This ministry we cannot do alone.

Our journey to justice often begins before we, as babies, can personally commit to the struggle for full inclusion. The community enters into this commitment on our behalf. The sacrament of Holy Baptism "is full initiation by water and the Holy Spirit into Christ's Body the Church" (BCP, p. 298). Our parents and sponsors promise to "seek and serve Christ in all persons . . . to strive for justice and peace . . . and respect the dignity of every human being" (BCP, p. 305). Later, through Confirmation, baptized persons are expected to "make a mature public affirmation of their faith and commitment to the responsibilities of their Baptism" (BCP, p. 412). What are the responsibilities of their Baptism? Paul, in the Epistle to the Galatians, reminds us that "when we have been baptized into Christ [and] have put on Christ" (Galatians 3:27–28), we must look at the world through new lenses, not seeing each other as Jew or Greek, male or female, slave or free, but as one family of Christ Jesus. That is what anti-racism and anti-oppression training seeks to do—to deconstruct the artificial barriers of race, class, ethnicity, and sexual orientation that make oneness impossible and to join with other people of God to reconstruct a world built upon the rock of unity that is in Jesus Christ our Savior.

In 2003, after sponsoring a successful anti-racism training program throughout the Episcopal Church, the Anti-Racism Committee of the Executive Council decided to commission works on anti-racism in the church for use in congregations. Though the training program has influenced many people, the committee hoped to prepare resources that would be suitable for adult education, whether or not the participants ever attended a training session. This book of short essays by notable authors from the Episcopal Church is designed to assist adults, as individuals or in groups, discuss racism from the perspective of different aspects of our faith. The discussion questions at the end of each essay are only a starting point of reflection and action in a parish. A Bible study resource focusing on racism, *Journeys and Diversity*, is also being published for parish use. With the support of Morehouse Publishing and publisher Debra Farrington, it is our hope that these additional resources will strengthen the overall anti-racism program of the Church.

May God, who has given us the will to work for a just world, give us the strength and determination to create models within our beloved church for the communities in which we live. I hope that this book serves as a beacon to light the way for us to achieve this goal.

Faithfully,
The Rev. Jayne J. Oasin
Social Justice Officer
Episcopal Church
Ash Wednesday, 2005

1   A DANGEROUS BOOK THE BIBLE

Frederick Houk Borsch

Frederick Borsch is Professor of New Testament and Chair of Anglican Studies at the Lutheran Theological Seminary at Philadelphia. The retired Episcopal Bishop of Los Angeles, he formerly was Dean of the Chapel at Princeton where he taught as Professor in the Religion Department and the Program in the History, Archeology, and Religions of the Ancient World, and was President and Dean at the Church Divinity School of the Pacific. His most recent book is *Keeping the Questions* (Cambridge, MA: Cowley, 2005).

When the subject is racism, the Bible is a dangerous book. Seen through racist eyes, the stories of what has been called the curse of Ham (Genesis 9:20–27) and the tower of Babel (Genesis 11:1–9) have been used to defend slavery in the United States, apartheid in South Africa, and the separation of races in these and other lands. The stories of the exodus and escape from slavery in Egypt and of return from exile have, on the other hand, been retold as exemplary narratives offering the divine promise to set oppressed people free. Jesus' parables and his suffering, death, and resurrection, along with the Spirit-led experiences of his first disciples, have brought consolation, hope, and courage to communities of people who have wanted to live without disfiguring distinctions of race or ethnicity, or, for that matter, gender, class, or even faith differences, and now, for many, sexual identity as well. Yet people are different, and those differences enrich life. But there is a strong human tendency to be fearful of what is different and often to equate "different" with "inferior." There are psychological reasons for putting others down, such as attempting to bolster self-esteem. When power equals economic advantage or other privileges, the powerful seek to be superior to others. Over the centuries religion has had a significant role in defining and establishing the distinctions between what is simply different and what is deemed to be inferior.

It is hardly surprising, then, that the Bible contains a complex series of stories about struggle and new understandings with regard to these issues. Part of this complexity results from the fact that many of the stories, and sometimes their interpretations and reinterpretations within the Bible, were told and retold over a long period of years. They come from somewhat differing cultures. They come from varying religions, in the sense that the interpretations, emphases, and practices in religion are always changing. Sometimes they do so in overlapping ways, as when a nomadic people slowly become more agriculturally based and then city-centered. At the heart of these "religions" of the Bible was worship of a God whose ways were not easy to understand. God's "thoughts are not your thoughts, nor are your ways my ways, says the Lord" (Isaiah 55:8). This God was a holy God of demanding righteousness and yet surprising mercy. Both these characteristics were true of God, sometimes seemingly at different times, but at other times at once! How were people to respond to such a God?

Another aspect of the complexity of the biblical stories is the awareness that they do not recognize race or racism in the ways in which people of later centuries would come to do so. In part this may have been a result of geographical separation. Although the peoples of the Bible lived with trade, travel, and migration, and were even depicted as migrant peoples themselves, they also lived at a distance from the peoples of China and the Far East. Peoples of more central Africa were known and play significant roles in the Bible but were not large enough in numbers locally to be thought about as a separate category of people. The peoples that were well known were a mixed lot of varying hues of tan and the products of a fair degree of migration and intermarriage among tribes. For many thousands of years, Israel/Palestine had been the major land bridge for ancestors migrating from Africa to Asia and Europe. The "Hebrew" peoples, though sometimes thought of as an ethnically distinct tribe, were, in fact, such a mixed group. The band of people who went to Egypt and then returned to the promised land were not just as they had been. They would have intermarried in Egypt—Moses had such a wife or wives, one of them likely central African[1]—and then mingled considerably with the local peoples among whom they came to live. To the degree that people could be distinguished into subgroups, it was largely by language and customs rather than by skin color and/or facial features. With respect to such customs, what people ate and how they chose to relate to one another in meal fellowship was of considerable importance.

But, first of all in the Bible, one learns that human life is created in the "image of God . . . male and female" (Genesis 1:27). All that this implies can be worked out in more than one way anthropologically and theologically, but it signifies that human life is in some ways like the divine (or God in some ways like us) in the capacities to think and to think about thinking, to be conscious and self-aware, then to have relationships, language, stories, responsibilities, and loves. All humans are descendants, and bear the image of, this first creation. This is a deep, underlying biblical understanding and is the basis for a kind of trajectory that continues to gesture its way through the whole of the biblical narrative.

Again, however, people are different, and the Bible contains a series of etiological stories (stories that tell of causes) that explains these differences. These stories tell how various peoples and nations are descendents from the name of a real or mythical person. Ham, for instance, was the youngest of Noah's three sons. One night, when his father was drunk and lay naked in his tent, Ham saw his father's nakedness and told his two brothers who managed to cover their father without seeing his nakedness (Genesis 9:18-28). In that time and place, it was a disgrace to see one's father's genitals and then tell of it. When Noah awoke, he blessed Japheth and Shem but cursed

Ham by the name of his son Canaan and, in one interpretation, thus his descendents. The shame of what Ham had done resulted in a curse that, by interpretation, helps to explain the later subjugation of the people of the land to the Hebrews. Because others of the sons of Ham are called Egypt and Cush (Genesis 10:6, the latter name sometimes associated with the people of more central Africa), racist interpreters of another millennium have used the story of Canaan's curse as a biblical warrant arguing for black inferiority and even for their slavery. Such misunderstanding of the biblical text and its misuse should be obvious. At most the story might be used to explain the supposed subjugation of the Canaanites of that land and times, and the curse, in any event, comes not from God but from the shamed and angered Noah.[2]

The tale of the tower of Babel (Genesis 11:1-9) is another explanatory story. How is it that the peoples of the known world are scattered about and have different languages? Once upon a time, so the story goes, there was but one language among a people living in the Tigris-Euphrates valley (the land of Shinar). They decided to build a great ziggurat-like tower that would become a kind of gateway to heaven. God saw this as a prideful attempt to exceed the limits of human life and even to usurp divine power. God, therefore, confused their language so that they could no longer understand one another and cooperate in such an enterprise. The story may "explain" why people of different languages cannot communicate well and why they have trouble cooperating, but this is seen as a result of human sin and not divine blessing. (When that biblical blessing does come in the form of the Spirit of Pentecost, people are able to communicate again and be in community in new ways.) The Babel story may seem to explain why languages and peoples are the way they are, but it offers no warrant for humans to further divide and separate themselves, much less to assume that one group is superior to another.

The Bible does, however, tell how the children of Israel came to see themselves as a special people. Perhaps most peoples do. Israel believed God had chosen them. This was not because of any special merit. Indeed, in a complicated and, one would have to say, stormy relationship with YHWH (often rendered as LORD), their God, the people of Israel frequently failed to live up to their calling. At times they believed themselves punished and even abandoned for their wrongs. Then the LORD would have mercy, and they could begin again.

At their best they saw themselves chosen for a kind of servant ministry. That God would choose a small and insignificant people for greatness demonstrated the greatness of God. The other nations would come to see the majesty of the LORD: not only that this was a superior God, but the only true God. Israel understood itself to be "a light to the nations" that would lead all other peoples to know and worship this true God.

The dangers in such a sense of special election are palpable, even if it is a matter of God's choosing and for a servant ministry. One recognizes, too, the dangers of monotheism (belief that there is only one God) or even henotheism (special relationship and worship of one God without necessarily denying the existence of others), if these beliefs lead to the suggestion that other peoples worship false or lesser gods. Other people may then seem less chosen. An ethnocentrism can be reinforced and grow as a religio-ethnocentrism—a highly developed concern for the special place of one's own group, strengthened by religious beliefs. Surely Israel was not alone in living with such dangers. She was also perhaps more aware of them than most.

The calling of this people of the LORD to be special and set apart was given its most forceful articulation in Deuteronomy and accompanying additions to other parts of the developing Hebrew Scriptures. Ascribed to the time of Moses, Deuteronomy (second law) was actually written in a later era when it was believed that it was important to reaffirm Israel's identity and calling: one of those periodic times when prophets and others felt that distinctive identity threatened. This may well have been during the reforms of Judah's king Josiah (encouraged by the prophet Huldah) in 621 BCE. There was then a renewed emphasis on allegiance and obedience to Israel's God alone, along with a warning about what would happen if the Israelites worshiped the gods of the local peoples. The temptation to engage in fertility rites, for instance, to try to ensure good crops and herds had to be utterly resisted.

The Lord your God you shall fear; him you shall serve, and by his
name alone you shall swear. Do not follow other gods, any of the
gods of the peoples who are around you, because the Lord your
God, who is present with you, is a jealous God. The anger of the
Lord your God would be kindled against you, and he would
destroy you from the face of the earth. (Deuteronomy 6:13-15)

In order to assure this degree of purity, God's people must have
nothing to do with the local peoples. The leaders of the deuteronomic reforms would hearken back to, and likely they rewrote, the
story of Saul's failure to utterly annihilate the Amalekites. (On other
struggles with the Amalekites, see Deuteronomy 25:17-19 with Exodus 17:8-15.) "Do not spare them, but kill both man and woman,
infant and suckling, ox and sheep, camel and donkey" (1 Samuel
15:3). Saul's disobedience of this edict brings about his rejection by
God as king. So one reads in Deuteronomy 7:1-6:

When the Lord your God brings you into the land that you are
about to enter and occupy, and he clears away many nations
before you—the Hittites, the Girgashites, the Amorites, the
Canaanites, the Perizzites, the Hivites, and the Jebusites, seven
nations mightier and more numerous than you—and when the
Lord your God gives them over to you and you defeat them, then
you must utterly destroy them. Make no covenant with them
and show them no mercy. Do not intermarry with them, giving
your daughters to their sons or taking their daughters for your
sons, for that would turn away your children from following me,
to serve other gods. Then the anger of the Lord would be kindled against you, and he would destroy you quickly. But this is
how you must deal with them: break down their altars, smash
their pillars, hew down their sacred poles, and burn their idols
with fire. For you are a people holy to the Lord your God; the
Lord your God has chosen you out of all the peoples on earth to
be his people, his treasured possession.

When, several generations later, Ezra and Nehemiah returned
with the remnant group from exile and were attempting to rebuild

Jerusalem and its temple, they took seriously the ban on intermarriage. Experiencing hostility from some of the local inhabitants, they extended the ban to include intermarriage with any non-Jews, including the Israelite people of the northern region who had intermarried (and would come to be called Samaritans). Judeans who were so married were ordered to put away their non-Jewish wives with their children. "Thus I cleansed them from everything foreign" (Neh 13:30).

Looking back, it may seem easy to criticize such xenophobia and "cleansing" by a people who believed they were doing God's will. Our concern, however, is less to make such judgments from the distance of time than to understand the peoples and circumstances of the period. So may we be aware of the dangers of interpreting the Bible in such a manner that attitudes and prohibitions from the past become ways of seeking to be holy in later times and circumstances. It is important to recognize, as well, that these deuteronomic strictures are just some among the Bible's many stories and teachings. There are other strands and traditions that in their ways undermine and, within the Bible, criticize, exclusivistic understanding of holiness. Once more we must recollect that trajectory, beginning from the first creation story, that knows the one creator God to be the God of all human life.

We should recognize, too, that these stricter forms of identity as a people were not, in their time, racist. They, in fact, had no realistic basis in ethnicity. There were no pure bloodlines or genetic pools, even if people could have thought in those terms. The children of the God of the Bible, now more limited to the people of Judea, were already well intermarried and, despite strictures, would continue to intermarry. Any idea that this people would keep themselves wholly separate was always a kind of fiction. One need only recall Moses' marriage or marriages to "foreign" women and the infamous story of David's sin with Bathsheba and against his loyal soldier Uriah (2 Samuel 11). Uriah was a Hittite, a member of one of the seven identified nations that had supposedly been exterminated (see Deuteronomy 7:2). He was married to Bathsheba, who might herself have been wholly or part Hittite. At least she was a woman of Judea who had intermarried. In any case, David took her as one of his wives, and their son Solomon (who, according to 1 Kings 11:1, "loved many foreign women") became a progenitor in the royal lineage.

In that lineage are other foreign women, among them Rahab, the harlot of Jericho (Joshua 2; 6:22-25), and the devoted Ruth, woman of Moab and great-grandmother of king David. These and other biblical narratives more than suggest that providence can be remarkably nonexclusive. These stories also follow that trajectory begun in the creation story and heard when Israel is reminded that it once experienced what it was like to be foreigners and strangers in another land. If they are to be a people of justice and holiness, they, therefore, must love even strangers or aliens as themselves.

When an alien resides with you in your land, you shall not oppress the alien. The alien who resides with you shall be to you as the citizen among you; you shall love the alien as yourself, for you were aliens in the land of Egypt; I am the Lord your God. (Leviticus 19:33-34)

That same trajectory may also be seen and heard in the wisdom books of the Bible, particularly Proverbs, Ecclesiastes, and Job. In part because similar teachings are found among other groups in the region, some of which were taken over into the Hebrew Scriptures, this is a wisdom that speaks more generally to the human condition.

A good name is to be chosen rather than great riches, and favor is better than silver or gold. The rich and the poor have this in common: the Lord is the maker of them all. (Proverbs 22:1-2)

A living dog is better than a dead lion. (Ecclesiastes 9:4)

Wisdom can be personified as a kind of attribute or partner of God, and the womanly figure of Wisdom or of a teacher of wisdom, together with the wisdom writings, seems to have had a significant influence on Jesus' teaching and ministry. In the Hebrew Scriptures, the understanding that the LORD God is the God of all people and the vision of an entire world at peace are related to the teaching of wisdom. Also related is the ideal of the servant Israel becoming a light to the nations that will ultimately enable God's salvation to "reach to the end of the earth" (Isaiah 49:6).

Many peoples shall come and say, "Come, let us go up to the mountain of the Lord, to the house of the God of Jacob; that he may teach us his ways and that we may walk in his paths." For out of Zion shall go forth instruction, and the word of the Lord from Jerusalem. He shall judge between the nations, and shall arbitrate for many peoples; they shall beat their swords into plowshares, and their spears into pruning hooks; nation shall not lift up sword against nation, neither shall they learn war any more. (Isaiah 2:3–4, paralleled in Micah 4:2–3)

Also linked to the wisdom tradition and a part of this greater vision and trajectory is the parody of the Book of Jonah. It is the tale of an unadmirable antitype of a prophet who does everything he can to avoid, and then to undercut, God's call to preach repentance to the foreign city of Nineveh (located in what is now Iraq). The hard-hearted and self-pitying Jonah ("I knew you are a gracious God and merciful," 4:2) just cannot get it through his thick head and heart that God can care about and forgive all these foreigners: "a hundred and twenty thousand persons who do not know their right hand from their left, and also many animals" (4:11).

Thus Jonah and other parts of the Bible that tell of God's care and concern for all life provide a reason for thoughtful people to read the whole Bible with anticipation while also retaining a certain hard-headed caution—even a kind of interpretive suspicion—with regard to how the Bible is sometimes interpreted and used. People that have been or are oppressed or marginalized (the poor, slaves, blacks, women, gay people, native peoples, and others) are aware of how those in power, or even just in the majority, have abused or can use portions of scripture to exclude or put down others. The Bible in its entirety is a complex web of stories and teachings brought forth out of many struggles to know God's ways for humanity. There are half steps and steps backward along the way. But there is also a momentum, seen as a trajectory and direction, then a vision of a new community, in which all people can live together with dignity and in harmony and peace.

Into these struggles to shape a new human community, Jesus was born. He grew up hearing and reading the Hebrew Scriptures,

and became a Jewish prophet and teacher of wisdom. His vision of
the reign of God in which all God's people would participate was
compelling. He believed that this movement (God's ways) was
already begun, seemingly in some special ways in his ministry. His
primary outreach was to those who could be considered to be outside the God movement. His anger was directed at those who would
exclude people they regarded as, for one reason or another, beyond
God's invitation: the poor, the maimed, those whose work or other
activities made them unclean. It was especially to these that Jesus'
ministry was directed: "I have come to call not the righteous but sinners" (Mark 2:17). "Blessed are you who are poor, for yours is the king-
dom of God. Blessed are you who are hungry now, for you will be
filled. Blessed are you who weep now, for you will laugh" (Luke
6:20–21). Even a rich and scandalous tax collector was beloved of
God: "Today salvation has come to this house, because he [Zaccha-
eus] too is a son of Abraham" (Luke 19:9).

Jesus seemed to have interpreted his healings and exorcisms of
evil spirits as indication that the new time foreseen by the prophet
Isaiah was at hand: "Then the eyes of the blind shall be opened, and
the ears of the deaf unstopped; then the lame shall leap like a deer,
and the tongue of the speechless sing for joy" (Isaiah 35:5–6). Those
whose handicaps might have been thought to be the result of sin
that excluded them from God's invitation were not beyond God's
reach or Jesus' touch. In varied parables, a number of them with a
remarkably similar inner theme, Jesus told of this surprising restoration and inclusion. At a dinner party "the poor, the crippled, the blind,
and the lame" will sit together at the table (Luke 14:15–24). The
prodigal son would be welcomed home and eat the fatted calf with
his friends, even if his older brother objected (Luke 15:11–32).
Twelve-hour workers would be paid the same as those who worked
only one hour and together be invited into a new basis of relationship one with another (Matthew 20:1–15).

In his disciples' eyes, Jesus "walked the talk." Several of his parables, such as the lost sheep (Luke 15:3–7) and the prodigal son, seem
to have been a kind of argument in defense of the invitation he
extended in God's name. "This fellow welcomes sinners and eats
with them" (Luke 15:2). But eat with them he did, and in story and

action, in word and deed, this remarkably free and open eating together was a demonstration and an enacted parable of new opportunity of acceptance and relationship.

Earlier I remarked that a number of Jews of Judea came to regard the people of Samaria as, at best, half-breeds. "Jews do not share things in common with Samaritans" is an accurate observation in the Fourth Gospel (John 4:9). But Jesus told a story about a remarkably kind Samaritan and asked the lawyer, whose question had prompted the parable, to imagine what it would be like to be desperately injured and then helped by someone one he had formerly looked down upon (Luke 10:25-37). Jesus offered healing to skin-diseased lepers and observed that the one who returned to give thanks was a Samaritan (Luke 17:16). He seems to have spent some of his ministry in Samaria and conversed openly, we are told, with a Samaritan woman (John 4:5-42). It would appear that Jesus' vision of the reign of God and the restoration it would bring included Samaritans. And, in a society of male privilege, it included women as well, some of whom seem to have been among his welcomed followers and early disciples, as well as exemplars in his stories.[3]

What of others? It may well have been that Jesus' initial vision of the God movement was for a restored and inclusive people of Israel: "I was sent only to the lost sheep of the house of Israel" (Matthew 15:24). Yet there are indications of his ministry breaking out and reaching to others during his lifetime. Although he seems to have struggled with himself, he heals the daughter of the Syrophoenician or Canaanite woman (Mark 7:24-30; Matthew 15:21-28). He responded to the centurion's plea to heal his slave (Luke 17:1-10; Matthew 8:5-13; see John 4:46-53). When criticized for taking upon himself the calling "to bring good news to the poor . . . to proclaim release to the captives and recovery of sight to the blind, to let the oppressed go free" (Luke 4:18 from Isaiah 61:1), Jesus rejoined with two stories from Israel's lore that tell of sustenance provided for a widow in Sidon and the healing of Naaman the Syrian (Luke 4:25-27).

After the death of Jesus, interpreted as a self-offering of God's reconciling love, and his resurrection, the invitation was to join into a new relationship with God through Jesus. He was understood to be the embodiment of the reign of God that he had proclaimed. He

had not only spoken God's word of forgiveness and new acceptance, he had enacted it. He was the Word of God. In his letters, Paul
does not speak of the reign of God as such. Nor does he retell Jesus'
parables or relate his stories of healing. Sometimes it is suggested
that there is a considerable gulf between Jesus' earthly ministry and
Paul's proclamation of him as the risen Christ. Yet at a deeper level
Paul seems to have had a profound grasp on the new relationship
with God and one another that Jesus articulated and embodied. As
the invitation to this new community spread to the Gentiles, Paul,
following Jesus, encouraged table fellowship and relationships without male-honor competitiveness. These relationships were more like
siblings at meal together. He insisted, against the counsel of Peter
and even his friend Barnabas, that there must be no reasons why
Jewish and gentile Christians could not eat together (see Galatians
2:11-21.) Hearers of the Bible learn more about similar issues in the
Acts of the Apostles (15:1-29), where a rather simple formula (avoiding food offered to idols or with the blood still in it, and unchaste
living) provided the basis for meals shared together by people of different backgrounds, customs, and taboos. More dramatic still is
Peter's vision of what seemed like a great sheet let down from
heaven on which there were all kinds of creatures (Acts 10:9-16). A
voice from heaven convinces Peter that God makes all things clean.
This enables the baptism of Gentiles and full community with them,
including shared meals. Doubtless this freedom included the sharing
of the meals of bread and wine as well, remembering and giving
thanks for the life, death, and new life of Jesus.

It was, Paul eloquently maintained, a new community without
privilege. No group or persons could have privilege over one another
because the invitation to membership was a free gift offered by God
through Jesus Christ. It was in this sense an end to religious privilege—even to religion, if seen as gaining privilege or advantage over
others. All were members of the body of Christ and, developing the
image with comic undertones, Paul notes that it would be ridiculous
in a body for the hand, the foot, the head, or the eye to try to enlarge
itself at the expense of other parts or to insist that it had no need of
the others (1 Corinthians 12:12-26). People are different, but they
now live in a new relationship and communion/community in which

"there is no longer Jew or Greek, there is no longer slave or free, there is no longer male and female." Gender or religion-based status or other ethnic, economic, or social conditions do not make a person more or less in this community, "for all of you are one in Christ Jesus" (Galatians 3:28).

In the Acts of the Apostles, Paul is said to have reached back to the creation story to offer to the Athenians an additional argument from a kind of natural theology: "From one [i.e., Adam] God made all nations to inhabit the whole earth" (Acts 17:26). In his Gospel's genealogy, Luke, the author of Acts, traces Jesus' lineage beyond Abraham to Adam. The story of the Acts of the Apostles is the story of the activity of the Holy Spirit directing the ministries of Peter, Paul, and others, and confirming the outreach of the good news in Christ Jesus to all the peoples of the known world. The fiery Spirit of Pentecost overcomes the language barriers of Babel (Acts 2:1-21). The long list of nations in Acts 2:9-11 demonstrates that no linguistic group, race, or people were excluded from the events of Pentecost. The Spirit tells Philip, who had been preaching in Samaria (Acts 8:4-13), to go and join the chariot of the minister of the treasury of the Queen of Ethiopia, as he rides from Jerusalem to Gaza reading from the prophet Isaiah (Acts 8:26-39). To this Nubian eunuch Philip offers "the good news of Jesus." Hearing this, and seeing some water nearby, the Ethiopian asks, "What is to prevent my being baptized?" Why not? Well, he is a Nubian, he is a foreigner, he is a eunuch! But none of this makes a difference in the Spirit. He is baptized and becomes emblematic of the new church to be in Ethiopia.

Problems and challenges remain. Although Paul believed the new relationship in Christ meant that Philemon should receive Onesimus "no longer as a slave but more than a slave, a beloved brother" (Philemon 16), the New Testament may seem too reticent on the issue of slavery. But the trajectory has been established. Women are often still left out or at times relegated to secondary roles in the Bible. But the trajectory is established. As the generations go forward, many Christian communities will sidestep and backstep, trying to turn being Christian into privilege: finding ways to regard other people as less worthy and not fully acceptable, not least because of race. They will even use scripture as a prop. Perhaps more challenging yet, Christianity itself will come to be viewed as a privileged religion whose members alone are acceptable or at least specially privileged with God—ahead of those of differing religions with their cultures, ethnicities, and races. Yet even in this, a trajectory has been established: "He is our peace; in his flesh he has made both groups into one and has broken down the dividing wall, that is, the hostility between us ... that he might create in himself one new humanity" (Ephesians 2:14, 15). The reconciling love of God, which Christians know best in Christ Jesus, can overflow all boundaries, even those of religion, and be a trajectory that extends to and includes every human created in the image of God and who, therefore, is fully brother and sister in the community of life.

Questions for Discussion

1. As you reflect on your own knowledge of the Bible, what are some passages or stories that touch on the themes of inclusivity or exclusivity? What do you think is the message, in biblical times and for people today?

2. Borsch refers to differences between people as a way to enrich life. In your own life, when have you experienced the differences between yourself and another as enriching? When have you experienced difference to be a source of fear or uncertainty?

3. If our church and society lived into Borsch's vision of "the one creator God" as "the God of all human life," how would we look or act? How does your vision of church and society today compare with this vision?

4. How do you believe that race and racism have shaped the way we interpret the Bible?

5. What biblical images of God and/or God's work among humankind suggest ways for our communities to confront racism?

2 BAPTISM

Liberating Sacrament of Identity and Justice
Fredrica Harris Thompsett

Fredrica Harris Thompsett is the Mary Wolfe Professor of Historical
Theology at the Episcopal Divinity School in Cambridge, Massachusetts, where she also served as Academic Dean for fourteen years. With
over thirty years of teaching experience in Episcopal seminaries,
Thompsett is a popular speaker and writer on topics related to baptism and ministry. The author of numerous books and articles, she is the
co-editor of *Deeper Joy: Lay Women and Vocation in the Twentieth
Century Episcopal Church* (Church Publishing, 2005).

How does baptism inform the Episcopal Church's contemporary
commitments to anti-racist, multicultural living, and ministry? What,
specifically, has anti-racism work to do with the sacrament of baptism? These are good questions, ones that I hope you will explore
with me in this chapter. The Bible (NRSV) and 1979 Book of Common Prayer will be primary resources for this inquiry. Along the way
I encourage each of us to think more deeply about baptism and its
relation to our shared identity as Christians. I invite you to embrace
those theological qualities of justice and hope that are inherent
within the identity of the baptized. Throughout our lives and day to

day, I believe that Holy Baptism invites and enables us to see one another lovingly as God's own, face to face.

What, then, has anti-racism work to do with baptism? Many of our earliest ancestors knew how to respond in faith to this pointed question. Their terminology, of course, would have been different, yet they would have connected work for justice with being among those beloved by God. They experienced and knew about oppressive divisions, with one group of people holding power over another. They knew about slavery, about a world where one person owned another's labor, and they lived in a distinctly multicultural world. They regularly told and preserved stories about unjust practices and conflict across harsh divisions of class, sex, race, and culture. I have in mind the righteous fury of the prophet Amos as he railed against those who sold the poor for a pair of shoes (Amos 2:6), or the haunting story in the Gospels about Lazarus and the poor man at the gate (Luke 16:19–31). Jesus is clear in the Beatitudes about those who are favored by God. "Blessed are those," we read, "who hunger and thirst for righteousness, for they will be filled" (Matthew 5:6). If we are tempted to think that faithful living exists only among folks who look just like us, then we will have to work to catch up with the wisdom of those faithful ancestors who preceded us in biblical times.

You still may be asking yourself: what does *baptism* in particular have to do with healing social divisions and with seeking justice in the world? Here is the key. At the heart of baptism, as our Christian ancestors knew it, is the biblical tradition of liberation. The ancient Hebrew prophets' messages of justice—particularly for the least, the lost, and the left out—were ingrained in their consciousness and identity. In the early centuries of Christianity, choosing to be baptized was risky. For most it took courage, for some it was life-threatening. After they completed a long period of study, candidates for baptism (they were called "catechumens") were named and identified as Christ's own, and not the Emperor's. The newly baptized were one in the Body of Christ, united by disciplined witness and service. Themes of liberating identity as God's beloved ones, of commitment and courage as disciples of Christ, and of hope for a just and peaceful future were deeply woven into their understanding of baptism.

Look with me for a moment at a telling verse from the Apostle Paul, a verse that many scholars now believe was an important part of early baptismal services: "As many of you as were baptized into Christ have clothed yourselves with Christ. There is no longer Jew or Greek, there is no longer slave or free, there is no longer male and female; for all of you are one in Christ Jesus"(Galatians 3:27–28). Paul presents baptism as overcoming all that alienates and separates human beings from one another and from God. Baptism sets aside all prior identities and offers unity and freedom in Christ. Baptism, now as then, builds the body of Christ from diverse peoples, races, and nations. Racism clearly violates the unity Christ gives us in baptism. Baptism both embraces differences and unites a liberated humanity as God's own.

Now, as then, new believers are born anew in Christ and dispersed, as at Pentecost, to be God's people at work in the world. Baptism is the foundational sacrament for all Christians and for all those who wish to convert to Christianity. Today in the Episcopal Church, the baptisms of those from other Christian denominations are honored and welcomed, for we are all baptized into Christ's one body. Some of you may have been baptized as Roman Catholics, Presbyterians, Baptists, or as members of other churches. What unites us all is that we are all God's own. Emphasis upon a broadly inclusive and welcoming missionary church is not a newfangled, contemporary idea. It is as fundamental as the witness of Jesus, and as expansive as the teaching of Paul.

I must admit that the impact of baptism was not clear to me or probably to my parents at the time of my baptism. Certainly, I am not alone in this regard. The themes of a liberating identity, of having the courage to struggle for justice, and of hope for a future resembling God's just reign on earth were not central in my memory. I do, however, literally remember my baptism! I was eight years old. My twin brother and I were privately sprinkled one Sunday afternoon in May with water from a small Gothic-style baptismal font that was hidden away at the very back corner of our vast, well-endowed, suburban parish church. The baptismal font, I recall, resembled a graceful birdbath. We stood quietly with half a dozen family members as the service from the 1928 Book of Common Prayer was accomplished in less than ten minutes. I also remember receiving a Prayer Book and a bright yellow Kodak Brownie camera. Later on I would learn to follow along in Prayer Book services, but at the time I soon put the camera to use taking family pictures. This was not a risky or courageous community event; rather, it was quite an enjoyable small, family party.

That was more than fifty years ago. How was I to know that the promises made by me and my godparents on that day would carry us forward in the years ahead in renewing and demanding ways? Across the decades I have learned more about wading deeply into the waters of baptism. Baptismal promises made or taken at any age hold potential for a life-giving future. I have come to appreciate the baptismal wisdom of my biblical ancestors, including their messages of liberating identity, of courageous struggles for peace and justice, and of persistent hopefulness in daily living. Along with many others, I am committed as a Christian to work day by day for a world where human beings are freed from alienation and separation and are able together to celebrate the love of God. In short, we are coming to appreciate the sacrament of baptism as a gift from God that "keeps on giving."

What prompted changes in baptismal practices? How has our theology of baptism changed over time? What does it mean "to live into" our communities? The short answer is the 1979 Book of Common Prayer. The longer response is related to regular worship in parishes where the authority and witness of the baptized are more commonly appreciated and to discussions in adult education classes. Today in the Episcopal Church we are blessed with a Prayer Book that pays more attention to baptism as a foundation for Christian living. We are not the only denomination that has renewed its public commitment to baptism. Influenced by the liturgical renewal movement during the second half of the twentieth century, Episcopalians and other Christians restored baptism to liturgical prominence with a renewed emphasis on this sacrament as a focus for shared religious identity.

A second component of this ecumenical renewal movement has theological consequences. The Episcopal Church as well as some other denominations are moving away from patterns that obscure the fact of God's goodness in creation. New Testament scholar Bill Countryman aptly reminds us that baptism affirms and interprets

God's good gift of life bestowed in creation. I am reminded of the
Prayer Book Collect for Ash Wednesday that points to a merciful God
who in creating "hate[s] nothing you have made." Ecumenically—as
affirmed in the World Council of Churches' 1982 text *Baptism,
Eucharist, and Ministry*—most Christian theology has shifted away
from an earlier emphasis upon original sin, including the supposed
sinfulness of a newborn child. Instead, baptism affirms new life in
Christ who hears our prayers of repentance and repeatedly offers
forgiveness of sins. Today the pastoral emphasis in baptism is upon
promises taken and on our future commitments. Typically we no
longer ask, as many did in days past, "What happens if the infant dies
before being baptized?" In most instances today we might find ourselves asking the question, "What will the ongoing life of the newly
baptized look like?" Today the baptismal promises we regularly
affirm in parishes hold life-changing implications.

Where will everyday Episcopalians see and experience these
changes? Signs of this liturgical renewal are clear in the 1979 Book
of Common Prayer's emphasis on Holy Baptism as public, community celebrations rather than as private, family affairs. The services
are normally intended to be part of Sunday parish services. They are
especially appropriate when a bishop is present and for such obser-
vances as the Easter Vigil, Pentecost, and All Saints' Day. Whether the
candidate for baptism is an infant, a youth, or an adult convert, baptism is a community-wide sacrament. Practical steps reinforce this
reality. If feasible, baptismal fonts are being placed, replaced, or
moved to more central and visible locations. The Prayer Book also
suggests that clergy, sponsors, and candidates face outward toward
the congregation so all may have "a clear view of the action," so we
may see and experience our diversities face to face. These and other
steps are taken to make sure that the administration of the sacrament of Holy Baptism and its symbolic actions are as clear, visible,
and participatory as part of the celebration of the Holy Eucharist.
Today all members of the parish—sponsors, parishioners, and all
who witness these vows—respond often with a loud, cheering shout
of "We will," signifying the community's agreement to support the
newly baptized. In today's Episcopal service of Holy Baptism, all
gathered are then invited to renew and affirm their own baptismal

promises. At this time we express our shared and liberating identity in Christ, as well as our willingness to seek God's mission in our lives and in this multicultural society.

Although there are resources scattered throughout the Prayer Book and Bible, I wish to focus in particular on the creedal affirmations and five promises made and renewed in the baptismal covenant. ("The Baptismal Covenant" may be found on pages 304–5 of the 1979 Book of Common Prayer.)

It is important to recognize from the start that the baptismal covenant begins with the people's threefold affirmation of who God is, as stated in the language of the Apostles' Creed. The "almighty creator of heaven and earth" is affirmed as the prime mover of humanity, the Triune God who creates, chooses, forgives, trusts, and pursues us. This biblical God of our ancestors is the active, loving One who seeks to be in relation with us. This is what a biblical "covenant" is— a response to God's initiating love. If we are tempted to think of God only as a private resource for our solitude, we are missing the central biblical message of a mighty God who is actively engaged in the affairs of the world. God is at work in society, present in our lives whether we wish it or not. Biblical scholar Walter Brueggemann once noted that this God "chooses to dwell with folks like us who have not made up our minds." It is significant that the baptismal covenant begins by inviting all present in the congregation to remember who God is by recalling the words of the Apostles' Creed. Baptism is more than a technical step related to becoming a church member. It is the community's affirmation of God in Christ.

As we reconsider and renew our understanding of baptism, the Prayer Book emphasis is based on God's hopeful desire to make a covenant, to relate to humanity. The sacrament of baptism is not simply or only about an individual decision. It is about God acting and the community of faith responding. Baptism calls forth our responsiveness. Yet how might we shape this responsiveness in our daily lives? The baptismal covenant helpfully proceeds by naming, and seeking our willingness to pursue, five specific directions for faithful living. One priest aptly calls these five promises "the consequences of faith in daily living."[1] There are various ways of summarizing these five questions to which all are invited to respond. Here is a one-sentence summary: baptized persons are urged to pursue formation, repentance, proclamation, service, and the search for justice and peace. With combating racism in mind, we might be tempted just to focus on the last question, the one that seems most relevant for shaping our efforts to dwell in a just society where all are respected. Yet it is important to focus on all five of these questions, exploring the promise each one holds for embracing anti-racist, multicultural living.

The first question is: "Will you continue in the apostles' teaching and fellowship, in the breaking of bread, and in the prayers?" This is a good place to start, for it reminds us that we are a fellowship, a community with strong ties to one another. A positive response to this question signifies our willingness to keep on learning, praying, studying scripture, and worshiping together. Here the people of God not only share in public worship and private prayer, but we commit ourselves to continue our education in the faith. When we study the Gospels, for example, we will find various stories of Jesus' baptism. Together they tell of God's loving and initiating action, of the gifts of water and of the Holy Spirit, and of our Savior rising up from the waters to commence God's mission in the world. Verna Dozier, one of the most provocative encouragers of baptismal ministry among laity and clergy, insists that "religious authority comes with baptism."[2] Baptism signals that God has given us, as covenanted partners, important work to do. In addition to study, prayer, and worship, this promise can and should be read as including education about anti-racism and other contemporary barriers that keep us from living up to God's expectations for us. I know, especially from the anti-racism workshops where I have participated, that this is typically hard and demanding work for many of us. It involves unlearning patterns that have divided us and growing in awareness about how our unearned privileges—in my case as an affluent, white woman— allow systemic oppression to continue. "Continuing in the apostles' teaching and fellowship" commits us to a life of discipleship. In our response to this first question, we pledge ourselves as a community to replenish ancient and modern resources for the journey ahead.

The strong language of the second question is arresting: "Will you persevere in resisting evil, and, whenever you fall into sin, repent and return to the Lord?" This question directly acknowledges the reality both of systemic evil and of individual sinfulness. It summarizes in one question, addressed to everyone in the congregation, the baptismal candidates' previous renunciations of evil, including "the evil powers of this world" and "all sinful desires."This question acknowledges a world marred by violence and oppression. It calls upon us to recognize our needs for personal and for social transformation. It requires an active, not passive, response in seeking repentance for our sins. It commits us to strive against evils that mar our common life. Some contemporary observers envision baptism as a sacrament of struggle and resistance.[3] Dr. Martin Luther King Jr. often quoted words attributed to Edmund Burke: "The only thing necessary for the triumph of evil is for good men to do nothing."The opportunity to resist, as Dr. King and others of our ancestors well knew, can be embraced as a liberating gift of freedom and hope. An affirmative response to this question puts the obligation to respond to evil and sin directly in our hands. Thankfully, the response the Prayer Book provides for this and all five questions is: "I will, with God's help."

The third question invites us to be proclaimers of God's word: "Will you proclaim by word and example the Good News of God in Christ?"This question reminds us that scripture for Christians is our primary language, our shared native tongue. Here we are invited to share its lessons in word and deed. Through his teaching, Jesus strengthened those who were called to follow him that they might seek others who would join in pursuing God's dream for humanity. For the Apostle Paul and many others who followed, this teaching involved sending out disciples to teach amid new cultures, lands, and peoples.We hear lessons from scripture Sunday after Sunday, and many Episcopalians also engage in intentional Bible study. All of this is indeed Good News. The pointed question from the baptismal covenant asks what will we do *after* we hear God's liberating message. I know that for many adults the verb *proclaim* suggests the formal activity of preaching. Yet pulpits are not the only way stations for evangelists. This question in the baptismal covenant suggests that the primary place of proclamation for the baptized is our everyday settings, our daily lives.

"Will you seek and serve Christ in all persons, loving your neighbor as yourself?"This fourth question in the baptismal covenant is another pointed and decidedly scriptural call to service. It recalls and paraphrases the great commandment: "You shall love the Lord your God with all your heart, and with all your soul, and with all your mind, and with all your strength" and "You shall love your neighbor as yourself"(Mark 12:30, 31). As my Massachusetts colleague in ministry Byron Rushing once observed, the request here is not for volunteers. What is intended is a decision to be God's people at work in loving ways in the world. Verna Dozier bluntly asks, "Do you want to follow Jesus? Or are you content just to worship him?"[4] This is a clear call to discipleship, to service in the world. The calling to the baptized is not a private event nor is it for the faint of heart. Loving our neighbors may prove difficult, loving our enemies may well prove costly. Desmond Tutu repeatedly reminds audiences today of a lesson he learned in the long struggle against apartheid in South Africa. The people of God are meant to be Godlike, Tutu says, and we show this in particular by loving our enemies. In recent years, the Episcopal Diocese of Washington, D.C. described itself as a community where "all are accepted, and none are despised." Membership in the community of the baptized is not about being a club or a gated community. Seeking and serving "Christ in all persons" is an expansive, encompassing promise.

This call to service prepares us for a fifth and summative promise. This last question builds upon each of the preceding affirmations in the baptismal covenant and lifts up the biblical vision of justice: "Will you strive for justice and peace among all people, and respect the dignity of every human being?" A few years ago, the seminary where I teach commissioned tee-shirts with its logo printed on the front and this baptismal question printed on the back. People in grocery checkout lines would stop and inquire appreciatively where this saying came from. The Apostle Paul would have been pleased, I believe. This fifth affirmation recalls his vision of God's expansive love for humanity, his willingness to cross-cultural boundaries. This call to respectful dignity directly attacks personal and societal prejudice, conscious and unconscious ways of separating ourselves from others. The implicit, positive message in this commitment to "respect the dignity of every human being" is that cultural diversity discloses God's creativity. Within the Anglican tradition, nineteenth-century

British theologian F. D. Maurice taught that God's redemptive love was intended for all, including those of other religions. A Jewish rabbi working on issues of religious pluralism observed that although he believed God chose the Jews, who is to say that God could call only one people. In God's realm, differences are to be valued, appreciated, and embraced as the people of God strive for peace and justice, locally and globally. This is a boundless promise.

Each and every one of these five promises has costs and consequences. They set forth daily challenges for the people of God. Actually putting these words to use may seem impossible unless we remember the context in which we make, and repeat, these affirmations. Baptism affirms most of all that we belong to God. God in Christ has elected to dwell among us. I am using plural words here intentionally. Faithful baptismal living, day by day, is a collective adventure. Roman Catholic theologian Hans Küng appropriately quipped that "the ticket to heaven is a group ticket." Anthropologist Margaret Mead observed and exhorted her colleagues not to "doubt that a small group of thoughtful, committed citizens can change the world." It is important that you and I remember that we are members of a beloved community, created, called, loved, and pursued by God.

Thinking about baptism as a plural sacrament contradicts prior notions of baptism as a private event. In this chapter we have reviewed biblical and liturgical ways that direct our renewed attention to baptism as a shared commitment to Christ. Embracing baptism as a shared commitment in our North American society is also countercultural. Andy Couch, a young theologian who is attentive to the church's future in this culture, writes these important and provocative words: "And yet baptism could be the church's most powerful response—perhaps its only response—to individualism. We who are baptized are no longer our own; we belong to God (Romans 14:7-8). In belonging to God, we belong to the other members of the body."[5] Belonging to God and thinking about Christ's commitment to us helps us more accurately envision baptism as a shared and divinely empowered identity. Couch observes that baptism holds the power to help us challenge the autonomous individualism and self-aggrandizing consumerism that are prevalent in much of contemporary society.

As the promises made and renewed in baptism become more real to us, baptism holds the potential to make us disciples who genuinely practice God's just and loving ways. Baptism charts our daily work as a people of God. While I don't have specific step-by-step actions to suggest in addition to those given directly in the baptismal covenant, I do have some clues to offer. The first clue I have already emphasized. Like our earliest Christian ancestors, it remains important to remember the collective nature of community of the baptized. Perhaps this is one of the reasons Dr. King repeatedly reminded those who traveled with him that they were members of the "beloved community."

Both Dr. King and Archbishop Desmond Tutu have proclaimed the responsibilities of liberated people to embrace love as an active force that requires conscientious religious practice. The contemporary spiritual author Kathleen Norris defines sin in the New Testament "as the failure to do concrete acts of love." What I am suggesting is that faithful living invites us to think about daily activities and actions, rather than focusing on roles and careers. This is one reason that, instead of speaking about "lay ministry" or "ordained ministry," I prefer to speak about "baptismal ministry" as a shared identity. All of us who profess membership in Christ's body have work to do. Among the baptized, as Paul reminds us in 1 Corinthians 12:4–11, there is a wide variety of gifts for ministry. It is important not to assume that some occupations or activities have more room for ministry than others.

The process of making difficult choices is another way of working toward God's compassionate ways. When I am stuck or blocked by guilt or fear, I wonder what this indecision says about my understanding of God and of others. When I am able to move forward, I try to remember to pause and consider how these actions are a response to God working through me. Reflective intentionality is part of embodying baptismal ministry. Whatever your daily activities or employment, consider asking yourself these three questions: Where do others and I need to be challenged? Where do others and I need to be comforted? Where might others and I work for the larger, common good?

We can practice our baptismal promises on a large or small scale. A diocesan colleague, who repeatedly prompts the Episcopal

Church to address the global HIV/AIDS pandemic, sees his baptism as a reminder that we are summoned to be sent out into a troubled world. A close friend, once an active consultant who traveled throughout the Episcopal Church, spent her last years housebound in a wheelchair and dedicated her remaining efforts to intercessory prayer. I met a woman a few years ago from rural New Hampshire who had what she described as a thoroughly mundane, mechanical job: entering actuarial data. Yet in her workplace and in her home she labored throughout the week to express her baptismal vows. She told me that she invented a baptismal bumper sticker: "Thank God It's Monday."

Parishes as well as people can express themselves as change agents for the common good. A 2001 survey by the Alban Institute revealed that those congregations who were active in social justice and community ministries were likely to be growing. This can also be true of those parishes that choose to work intentionally on multi-cultural and racial hospitality, or on addressing systemic issues of injustice in the public square. Faculty colleague Christopher Durais-ingh describes the creative struggle of baptismal commitment as a movement from inward-looking passivity to outward and active engagement in seeking God's will. For the baptized, the central mes-sage of the Gospel is *not* just that we should go to church devoutly, read the scripture regularly, and show up whenever it feels good. The call to the baptized is that God relies on us to do God's work, that God in Christ came among us to affirm that message, and that the Spirit of God is upon us to take up this work.

I began this chapter by pointing to the biblical tradition of libera-tion that grounded our ancestors' understanding of baptism. Today we might translate this concept of liberating identity into such reli-gious expressions as being liberated to worship together, sent out to witness to God's love in the world, and released to serve God's dream of peace and justice. With the generosity of God's love offered to us in the sacrament of baptism and reaffirmed in the baptismal covenant, we are freed up to take risks, to challenge such pernicious realities as racism and other imbedded social evils that wrongly alienate us from one another. Remembering our shared responsibilities as a liberated people, we will be blessed to see the face of God in each other.

Questions for Discussion

1. What is your "baptism" story? If you were baptized as an infant and have no personal memory of the occasion, what other story related to baptism holds meaning for you?

2. Reflect on the Baptismal Covenant in the Book of Common Prayer (pages 304–5). What themes and promises stand out for you? How do you feel they relate to seeking justice in the world?

3. Thompsett writes, "Holy Baptism invites and enables us to see one another lovingly as God's own, face to face." What does this sentence suggest to you? How does it relate to healing social divisions? How does it relate to race and racism?

4. How do you experience your daily activities and actions as ministry? How do you follow Jesus in the world today? What are the implications of this call for you?

5. We live in a world today where there are many divisions between people of faith. For you, what is the role of the baptized Christian in a pluralistic world?

3

EUCHARISTIC RECONCILIATION

Michael Battle

Michael Battle lived in residence with Archbishop Desmond Tutu in South Africa for two years, 1993–1994, and was ordained a priest by Tutu in 1993. Michael has written out of his studies and friendship with Desmond Tutu, including such books as *Reconciliation: The Ubuntu Theology of Desmond Tutu* (Pilgrim Press, 1997) and *The Wisdom of Desmond Tutu* (Westminster John Knox, 2000). His latest book *Blessed Are the Peacemakers: A Christian Spirituality of Nonviolence* was recently published by Mercer University Press. Battle has also co-authored a book with Tony Campolo entitled *The Church Enslaved: A Spirituality of Racial Reconciliation* (Fortress Press, 2005). His most recent book is *Practicing Reconciliation in a Violent World* (Morehouse, 2005). He is currently Vice President, Associate Dean of Academic Studies and Associate Professor of Theology at Virginia Theological Seminary in Alexandria, Virginia.

The light shines in the darkness, and the darkness did not overcome it. (John 1:5)

We often read this prologue from the gospel of John with a hidden bias that darkness is inherently evil. Such an assumption is common; for example, those of my generation who grew up at the end of the 1960s grew up with evil cartoon characters painted black. Unfortunately, the association of evil and blackness is not just common to western cultures. When I spent four months in India, I noticed that the antagonists in movies are often African or dark skinned. How do we see the face of God in each other, if the other is black?

A thirty-four-year-old white woman sat down in her office to take a psychological test called The Implicit Association Test. Just by looking at her pictures on the wall, one could notice right away that the woman had a passion for civil rights. She was a senior activist at a national gay rights organization. Fighting bias and discrimination was what got her out of bed. The woman took a test on her computer from Harvard University's website.[1] It was a simple test to distinguish between a series of black and white faces.

When she saw a black face, she hit a key on the left, and when she saw a white face, she hit a key on the right. Next, she had to distinguish between a series of positive and negative words. Words such as *glorious* and *wonderful* required a left key; words such as *nasty* and *awful* required a right key. The test then required the combination of the two categories. The activist hit the left key if she saw either a white face or a positive word, and hit the right key if she saw either a black face or a negative word.

Then the groupings were reversed. The woman's fingers furiously worked the keyboard. She now had to group black faces with positive words, and white faces with negative words. This made her concentrate more and work harder. She made no mistakes, but it took her longer to sort through all of the words and images. Her results appeared on the screen, but she was not pleased. This social activist became silent as her test found she had a bias for white faces. The woman concluded, "It surprises me I have any preferences at all. . . . I'm progressive, and I think I have no bias."[2]

The light shines in the darkness, and the darkness did not overcome it.

When we look for God's face, we are trying to remember another reality beyond ourselves. It may seem strange to think that we must "remember" God, but this is precisely what occurs when we seek the face of God in each other. Ancient Christian mystics like Dionysius and theologians like Thomas Aquinas teach us that human beings cannot know God without mediation. Only a few mystics obtain direct, intuitive knowledge of God. Most of us need some kind of mediation in order to recognize that it is God we've encountered. We need a reference point to discern what is of God. And so, once we reflect upon the reference point, we then remember God in our midst. This is where darkness can become a good thing because God's direct revelation would blind us. We need God to reveal God's self to us slowly and intelligibly, so that we understand when God is present. God must become dark for us to see God's face.

We must remember that everything dark is not evil. We need darkness to rest, to grow in our mother's womb, and most of all to know God. The Psalmist states: "If I say, 'Surely the darkness shall cover me, and the light around me become night,' even the darkness is not dark to you; the night is as bright as the day, for darkness is as light to you. For it was you who formed my inward parts; you knit me together in my mother's womb" (Psalm 139:11-13). The spiritual masters, Dionysius, and the spiritual director in *The Cloud of Unknowing* agree and instruct their disciples that God is only known in darkness. What an association—darkness and God. No one needs to do a Harvard study on how many western Christians usually tend to see God (i.e., white, European, male, and old). The spiritual masters taught us to resist stereotyping God for the sake of our very salvation. If we continue to make God into our own graven image, we run the risk of worshipping an idol. In other words, if we think we can clearly see God, most likely we are only seeing images of God made by human hands. This is why God's darkness is a good and counterbalances human tendencies toward idolatry.

The light shines in the darkness, and the darkness did not overcome it.

To God, darkness is not evil. The poet and songwriter James Weldon Johnson also gives us this deep insight:

And the darkness rolled up on one side,
And the light stood shining on the other,
And God said: That's good![3]

James Weldon Johnson imagines *the Adam*, dark from the mud of the riverbank, with God's breath in his lungs (Genesis 2:7). It's as if Johnson playfully imagines God in his own image: God is like a black man (up from the bed of the river God scooped the clay). Johnson's God seems to be like Bill Cosby, as Johnson imagines that God "batted his eyes, clapped his hands, And God smiled again." For many, James Weldon Johnson is on the verge of blasphemy, when he imagines a black God. And then, for feminists, Johnson's male God also gets in the way. But all of our associations of God are ridiculous, because none of them can completely describe God's reality. My wife told me recently of the conversation that she had in Spanish with our nanny. My wife, Raquel, meant to say, "Maria, please place Bliss's [our three-year-old daughter] broken toy in the trash." Instead, she ended up saying in Spanish, "Maria, after you place Bliss in the trash, please see about the broken toy." If we mean one thing in English and say the other in Spanish, how much more confused are our images of God? This is why God entreats us to constantly seek God's face in each other; no one image of God's face, seen in those around us, is sufficient.

Desmond Tutu's humor helps me explain:

Here are two stories which some of you may already know. The red Indians tell how in the beginning God created [human beings] by molding them out of clay. He put the first lot into the oven to fire them as is done with bricks and pottery in a kiln. He forgot about them. When he remembered and rushed to look in the oven he found a poor man burnt black—and that is the origin of the black races.

He placed another lot in the oven but they were underdone— and that was the origin of the white races. He put in the last lot which came out just right, neither over done nor underdone— that was the origin of the Red Indians.

The second story relates how God finished molding [humanity] out of clay. Then [God] said, "Go and wash in the pool down there." Some of this lot jumped into the stream and came out all white and clean—that was the white race. But the others feared

the water and just dipped the soles of the feet and the palms of
the hand in the water. They remained black all over except for
their palms and soles of their feet. Those needless to say were
the black races.

These two stories reflect the almost universal attitude to black
people, that somehow they are God's step children, hardly able
to hold their own in any sphere of competition with the non-
black races, with no really worthwhile achievements to their
name in the arts, in thought and least of all in religion.[4]

*The light shines in the darkness, and the darkness did not over-
come it.*
The Harvard study, James Weldon Johnson, and Archbishop Desmond
Tutu teach us that we need to unlearn our prejudices, not only for
the sake of being progressive and politically correct, but because we
may end up not believing in the living God who surpasses all that
we can imagine. When we fail to unlearn our prejudices, we often
end up worshiping a large image of ourselves and calling it God.

So, how do we unlearn our racial prejudices and open our imag-
inations to God? The Jesuit philosopher Teilhard De Chardin helps
explain how we may unlearn racial prejudice when he states: "By
virtue of the creation and, still more, of the Incarnation, nothing
here below is profane for those who know how to see."[5] For Christians today, there is no more important practice of learning how to
see God's face than through practicing the Eucharist.

The visible Church must eat, drink, pray, and worship together in
order to be a sign of "continuing vitality of the grace of Christ and of
hope for the redemption that he promises."[6] To see God's face in each
other, we must (re)discover eucharistic reconciliation, that miracu-
lous reality in which the Christian community (*sensus fidelium*) may
find overall agreement. God will be found not only in our images but
also in the image or our neighbor. This realization is crucial to both
the community and the individual in order to experience transformation into the divine life, so that we will one day behold the beatific
vision of God. But such hope, based upon eucharistic reconciliation,
will remain oblique if a Christian community is never transformed by
a natural sense of thankfulness for how God is revealed in our neigh-

bor. *Eucharist* literally means "thankfulness." The Eucharist makes us
thankful to find God's face in each other. If there is no sense of thankfulness in the individual believer, then that person is afflicted with
the worse kind of blindness, one that disallows sight of God.

The Trinity and the Incarnation provide the light to see how
God encounters us. It is in thankful interaction that God encounters
humanity. What the contemporary Christian must admit is that
among all declared sources of revealed authority of God there still
remains no direct access to God and the divine life. In other words,
you and I are still here on earth with fragmented thoughts and ideas.
We are not yet in heaven. As I once reflected with a friend while
watching the movie *The Exorcist*, if God's eucharistic presence were
taken seriously in the movie, the terror would become more like
slapstick comedy. The Christian must begin and end with the premise that Immanuel is true only in the face of the other who makes us
thankful for God's presence in our world.

*The light shines in the darkness, and the darkness did not over-
come it.*
Instead of limiting God, it would be a more fruitful task to remember that we, as human beings, see only as human beings, not as God.
The method that is needed in contemporary theology can be exem-
plified in the moral obligation of the Eucharist. The Eucharist shows
Christian revelation to be irrational unless that revelation somehow
fits in with our antecedent convictions. The mystery of the Eucharist
points to the current transformation of our beginning to discover
Christ for us in the other. Here, I am not thinking of what has
devolved into a lowest common denominator of some form of a
benevolent humanity; rather, I want to make clear that the Christian
conviction to remember Christ in the Eucharist is what facilitates a
vision of God. And it is in this conviction of the Eucharist that we
must acknowledge the limit of words in their attempt to describe
our way to truth in this world. By practicing the Eucharist with our
neighbor (and our enemy), we accept that the Incarnation will
always elude categories defined by us. The Eucharist provides an
alternative to the basic assumption in racism that depends upon the
dominant form of cultural revelation of God. And it is through the

Eucharist that we may see how to interpret effectively and apply the
teaching of Christian revelation to a suffering world. Thus the
Eucharist socializes the Christian community to seek the face of
God in each other, no matter who the other is. It is in the Eucharist
that it is theoretically possible to see and practice how the particular and the universal properly relate as one.

The moral controversies of the past, present, and the future cannot be resolved by appeals to more and better information at our dis-
posal. Such a natural law leads to the premise that Black American
slavery benefited the society at large due to the unfortunate limit of a
pre-technological age. This is the endemic racism that still creates categories of sub-humanity. In the Eucharist, a procedure exists that
refuses any category of subhumanity. Eucharistic reconciliation is a
model that shows itself neither as a relativistic theory nor a mono-
lithic structure, but as a Christian practice of the presence of God.
Jesus taught us to be eucharistic beings. If we are not eucharistic, then
we no longer have a reference point from which to see what is not of
God. But this need not be the case if one follows the gage of a thankful heart that seeks communion with God. To display the practices of
a thankful heart, we end where we began, with the Harvard study.

The Implicit Association Test is designed to examine how words
and concepts are strongly paired in our minds. For example, *lightning* is associated with *thunder*, rather than with *horses*, just as *salt*
is associated with *pepper*, *day* with *night*. We learn from this test
that the reason it is difficult for us unlearn prejudice is the same reason it is hard to associate lightning with horses or salt with night.
"Connecting concepts that the mind perceives as incompatible simply takes extra time."[7]

God's time is meant to be our time. That's why God enters our
suffering time and space. "I'm lonely still," God said. And "like a
mammy bending over her baby, kneeled down in the dust toiling
over a lump of clay till he shaped it in his own image."[8]

*The light shines in the darkness, and the darkness did not over-
come it.*
We unlearn our prejudices by helping God give birth in God's own
time. We counter stereotypes by developing close friendships with

those different from us. But this takes work and time. The researchers of the Harvard study concluded that working against implicit racism is "much like going on a new diet with healthier food. Just as healthy eating can have a subtle impact on how people look and feel, counter-stereotypical experiences sustained throughout one's life seem to subtly change how one thinks."[9] Mahzarin Banaji, one of three researchers who developed the Implicit Association Test, believes "that conscious efforts are needed to fight what she calls ordinary prejudice, the primitive brain filtering the world through its biased lenses without the conscious part of the brain being aware of it."[10] Banaji, of Indian descent, took the test and also favored white faces. Almost from the moment she discovered this, she applied her research to her own life. Her office at Harvard is testimony. You can see famous women and African-Americans all around: George Washington Carver, Emma Goldman, Miles Davis, Frederick Douglas, and Langston Hughes. She has learned to be thankful for these people in order to counter natural, racist tendencies. I call this thankful process eucharistic reconciliation.

As Christians, our very lives are to be eucharistic reference points that help us and others to break the patterns of prejudice in our lives. When people experience our character, there should be an expansion of worldview in which we remind everyone that God created us and that we did not create God. Our life as a frame of reference should liberate people from small worldviews and thereby create thankfulness. In short, we unlearn prejudice by making others thankful for our existence. Let our very lives help others move from suffering, to liberation, and finally to reconciliation in Christ, our continual hope.

Questions for Discussion

1. One of the key foci in Battle's article is his discussion of negative prejudice toward "darkness." Given this understanding of cultural bias, how would you interpret the passage from John 1:5: "The light shines in the darkness and the darkness did not overcome it"? What are some positive images of darkness?

2. When you hear the phrase "seeing the face of God in each other," what images and metaphors come to mind? How do you experience the face in God in your neighbor? How does Battle's essay affect your own view of God?

3. How do cultural factors shape our image of God?

4. Battle explains the Eucharist in the context of "a thankful heart that seeks communion with God." Reflecting on this insight, identify your own theology of the Eucharist. How does seeking communion with God relate to your commitment to anti-racism?

5. Drawing on your own knowledge of other races and cultures, describe the implications you see for eucharistic reconciliation and "seeing the face of God in each other."

4

RACE AND RECONCILIATION

Writing a New Ending to an Old Story
Steven Charleston

The Right Reverend Steven Charleston is President and Dean of Episcopal Divinity School in Cambridge, Massachusetts. The former Bishop of Alaska, he is the author of "Good News: A Congregational Resource for Reconciliation." He is a citizen of the Choctaw Nation of Oklahoma and has been active in justice ministries for indigenous communities and the environment.

Almost twenty years ago, I was asked to write an article on racism for a Christian periodical that is well known as a voice for the progressive Christian agenda. The magazine was *Sojourners* and my small essay was only one of many in a whole issue devoted to the subject of racism. In fact, my article was one of countless others that have appeared in print over the last two decades as theologians, community activists, and church leaders have continued the public debate on race relations in America. The articles keep coming because the problem never seems to go away. While I can not remember everything I wrote twenty years ago, I can remember the title *Sojourners* gave to their special edition on racism. It is a theme that seems to capture the perennial nature of racism in our society: "White Racism: America's Original Sin."

37

As I write yet another essay on racism, the irony is that we have made about as much progress on it as we have on original sin. We have many theories about how racism began, what it is, what it means, and what we ought to be doing about it, but the sin continues. Racism is alive and well in the America of this century, just as it was in the America of the last century. And the century before that. Like original sin, it seems to have marked us forever. It is a curse so indelible that Christian writers in the next century may still be recycling our lament that racism is a sin that can never be reconciled.

Perhaps faith can be defined as the ability to believe that racism can and will be redeemed. Perhaps it is a little like believing in miracles. Against all of the evidence, the community of faith must assert that no matter how resistant the sin of racism is to reconciliation, it is still not stronger than our capacity to forgive, to trust, and to love. Racism is powerful, subversive, adaptable, and deeply imbedded, but it is not invulnerable. There are strategies that can and do work against it. There are methods that overcome it, when applied with intention and intensity. There are ways to reconcile racism in America, in the Church, and in the world, and it is our task as people of faith to never despair of those strategies, even if it should take another thousand years for them to succeed.

It is in this spirit of faith that I come to the subject of racism once again. I come with confidence and hope born of faith, but with the pragmatism and humility of experience. In this brief look at racism and reconciliation, I will offer three simple sketches of our future. The first is a *premise* on which my understanding of racism is built; it is the scope of the task before us. The second sketch looks at three essential *issues* that define the strategies we must employ; they illustrate the priorities for the work we must do together. Finally, I offer a modest *proposal* that suggests a hopeful vision of our future; it is a proposal to end the cycles of our long national lament.

The Premise: Racism Is Culturally Pervasive

The title of the *Sojourners* magazine was "White Racism: America's Original Sin." Today, I would change that title. I would call it something like "Cultural Racism: America's Growing Sin."

I play with these words to intentionally shake us free from the kind of literal black-and-white thinking that was expressed in the *Sojourners* title of twenty years ago. Over the last century, the focus on white racism as the foundational core for racial oppression in our society slowly intensified in clarity and credibility until it helped to release the energy of the historic Civil Rights Movement. That movement was spearheaded by African-American leadership precisely because the power analysis of white racism was most vividly apparent against the backdrop of slavery, the compelling and convicting experience of America's black community. This very literal white/black cultural dichotomy was a crucial trajectory for efforts at reconciliation and justice. It brought us through the end of the twentieth century and laid the groundwork for the many other human liberation movements that grew in its wake.

Now, to both honor and sustain the struggles of the past, we need to broaden our focus. As we begin another century in combating racism, we must recognize that in a multicultural society, racism adapts and becomes equally multicultural. In other words, racism is pervasive in all of the cultures that make up contemporary America. If the movement to combat racism spread throughout all of our communities, so did the very thing we were fighting.

Asserting this, of course, is both controversial and challenging because it can seem to take the pressure off of the white community. Given the differential in power that white America wields in cultural relations, it is obvious that the greatest threat we face remains white racism. It continues to be America's original sin. But I would argue that we must expand our understanding of the breadth of racism, not in lieu of white racism, but because of it. White racism is becoming generic racism in America. Whether it makes us uncomfortable to acknowledge it or not, racism is now, and has been for some time, mutating into all of our cultures. In other words, if the white community is a carrier of racism, we have all caught the disease.

Racism today is culturally pervasive in America. Facing that reality is the great challenge before us all. Far from excusing or minimizing white racism, this fact will mean that we must place white racism in a context far more insidious and sophisticated than we may have acknowledged before. It will call for a much more subtle analysis than a simple equation of power. Tracing the threads of racism throughout the fabric of American life will require a degree of multicultural cooperation beyond anything we could have envisioned in the Civil Rights Movement of the 1960s. It will mean a willingness on the part of activist leaders to unify their efforts and sustain a common project across cultural lines: something that we have not been able to do in the last century to the degree that it will be necessary in this century.

For persons of color, the challenge will be to hold ourselves accountable for the ways in which racism is insinuating itself within our own communities. While we have been accustomed to thinking of racism in a two-dimensional context, we must now think of it as both an external and an internal threat across a wide spectrum of our own cultural values. We can not be successful in exposing white racism if we fail to reveal the growing levels of racism in our own communities. We must begin to recognize our own internalized oppression. We are not only becoming agents of our own undoing, but we are aiding and abetting racism against other communities of color. In short, we are subverting ourselves just when we need a unified front as never before.

Accepting racism as being pervasive does not let anyone off the hook. It expands the hook to make us all responsible for the part we play in perpetuating racism. Racism is not "their" problem; it is "our" problem. Our analysis must be multidimensional. Our strategies must be equally diverse. There are reasons that racism is a multicultural problem in America. Those reasons form the basis for the kind of social analysis we must do in the future, and they point us toward the unified strategies we must pursue. We will not stop the spread of racism in this century using the methods of the last century. Our response must be as pervasive and as adaptable as racism itself.

Three Issues for Reconciliation

Because racism exists within all American cultures, our strategies for dealing with it must be equally pervasive. We must identify the common ground that we all share in working against racism in a multicultural context. That means finding the sources of racism that are generic to all of our cultures. These will be opportunities for us to work together to effect reconciliation.

What are the dynamics of racism in this generation? How does it mutate across cultural lines? How is it spread and what can we do to uproot it internally while resisting it externally?

There are many answers we can give to these analytical questions about culturally pervasive racism. I will not pretend to be able to offer them all in this brief essay, but I will sketch three responses that suggest the scope of the work to be done within each cultural community and across cultural frontiers.

The first issue is the *transference* of racism through other forms of oppression. If we want to know how racism spreads through a culture, or from one culture to another, we should look to the web of human relationships that are the matrix of culture. The ways that members of any cultural group treat one another is a direct measure of how susceptible that group is to the growth of racism.

One of the most salient examples of this transference can be seen in the relationship between the genders. How men treat women in any culture is a powerful indicator of how permeable that culture is to racism. In simple terms, if men can disrespect women with impunity, and if they develop a deep pattern of doing so over a prolonged period of time, then a channel is formed that allows that same level of disrespect to be transferred to persons of another racial or ethnic community. Sexism breeds racism. Male-fixated styles of behavior in any culture not only oppress women, they produce the climate in which racism may grow. It is a short distance between treating females as unequal to treating people of other colors as unequal. In white culture, this correlation is often overlooked, just as it is in communities of color, but the principles are the same in any culture. The cultural inequality of men and women allows dehumanization to be transferred from gender to race. A man who believes women are inferior is more than capable of believing men of a different ethnicity are inferior. Sexism opens a point of transference and racism passes through, infecting the host culture and attacking neighboring cultures. It is not surprising, therefore, that if racism creates suffering, it is women and the children they nurture who suffer the most.

While sexism may be one of the most pervasive transference linkages in any culture, it is by no means the only one. Wherever there are distorted, dehumanizing relationships, there are points of transference for racism to take hold and grow. Homophobia, the status and treatment of both children and the aged, awareness to those with physical and/or mental challenges: all of these are transference vehicles for racism. A culture's immune system to racism is inevitably weakened if that culture practices intolerance toward its own homosexual community, brutalizes its children, disregards its elders, or ignores those with different levels of physical or mental ability. In short, these many relationships, which can be masked under the umbrella of cultural norms, are the points of entry for racism into a culture, and they are the points of infection where racist attitudes are passed throughout a culture. The way that we treat every member of our own cultural group has a direct impact on how healthy our culture is in fighting racism. If those relationships are distorted and oppressive, then the mutation of racist opinions and behaviors becomes much more likely over time. Consequently, in this century we can no longer afford to condone gender oppression, homophobia, child abuse, or the marginalization of our elders. Saying that this is how it is for us will not be acceptable. We will all have to be willing to confront those inherent points of transference for racism that exist within our cultures, the oppressions we practice against ourselves, and we will have to make the changes necessary even if it creates an internal backlash from our male populations.

The second issue we face is the *permission* we give to racism through our cultural understandings about competitiveness. Every culture has a value system related to competition. Often, these can be quite constructive and healthy. For example, the cultural value on academic achievement helps children in a competitive educational system. A cultural value on athletics can produce sports stars who are very successful competitors. In principle, these value-oriented styles of competition are positive and, if teamwork is involved, are actually inhibitors to the spread of racism.

There is, however, a hidden dimension to competitiveness. It is one we must expose and analyze as a prime conduit for racism, even though it means we must criticize an article of faith on which American society is built. The United States is a capitalistic society where competition in the market places is not only allowed but encouraged. The myth of the American Dream is the myth that every person can find economic success, even wealth, through hard work in an "open" market. To question this mythology, to question capitalism, is to question America. Without surfacing these assumptions, our strategies for dealing with the economic consequences of racism have been to put Band-Aids of work programs for the poor onto a system that we never truly challenge.

Economic competition is not the same as doing well in school or on the basketball court. There are rules that level the playing field in both the classroom and the sports stadium, but there are no rules between cultures when it comes to struggling for a piece of America's economic pie. In fact, the game is fixed. While capitalism pretends that all of the players have an equal chance of success, the reality is far different. White American culture has distinct advantages before the game even begins. Communities of color are handicapped even before they enter the competition. Therefore, communities of color find themselves not competing for larger slices of economic benefit, but forever smaller amounts of the leftovers.

Distorted economic competition creates the class struggle so historic to capitalist consumerism. As the degree of classism increases, as the competition becomes more intense, racism emerges as the by-product of an oppressive and unfair economic structure. For white American culture, this slanted economic competition means that racism is both profitable and beneficial. It provides access to privileges that are taken for granted and jealously guarded. There is far less incentive to change the status quo because racism pays dividends.

For cultures of color, this kind of competitiveness subverts the values of cooperation, solidarity, and compassion. It encourages a sense of rivalry that gives permission for racist attitudes toward others. Immigrant populations and/or undocumented workers are especially vulnerable in this atmosphere. The dominant class scapegoats these communities as being threats to economic stability while maintaining a class structure that is deeply racist and designed to keep others out of the circles of affluence and power.

Competition among the economic classes of American society gives permission for racism to exist, both within a culture and between cultures. It makes persons of a different race targets because they are perceived as being competitors. To "beat" them is the goal. This becomes especially virulent if the object of the competition is believed to be very limited. When communities of color know that they have only limited access to a source of economic advantage that allows a few to live in privilege while most live marginally, then the incubation of racism is almost assured. The men and women with whom they should be making common cause will be seen as threats, not allies. The hierarchies of class structures force human beings into competition for what should be theirs by right: decent housing, meaningful employment, responsive health care, and quality education. When these essentials are seen as being in limited supply, when access is made possible only through the elimination of rivals, and when class becomes equivalent to race, then racism is given a blank check by an economic system that supports it in a monopoly of power.

The third issue is the *integration* of racism into our cultures through the spiritual or religious values we profess. Of all of the areas of analysis for pervasive, multicultural racism, this is perhaps the most delicate and the most subtle. While we may be able to imagine that racism can enter into our cultural lives through oppressive personal relationships or distorted economic competition, it is harder for us to accept that those cultural institutions that represent spiritual life for us also embody a vehicle for the spread of racism. However, if we are sincere in evaluating how racism moves within any culture, then we must not withhold any aspect of that culture from our scrutiny. In other words, we cannot have any sacred cows, even if those cows are what we call our churches.

Religion plays an integrating role in culture. Faith systems take the human condition in all of its complexity and make sense of it through the medium of spiritual values and practices. We go to church, mosque, or synagogue to find meaning in our lives. We attend worship in order to keep our everyday lives in perspective, both with one another and with the God that we serve. At its best, religion is one of the most important advocates against racism because it provides a shared experience for believers of all races. It offers a message of self-worth, hope, and guidance to ground our relationships in ethical behavior. It holds up an ideal of love and justice that inspires us to work more passionately for the fulfillment of God's purpose in history.

And yet, even though it is a blessing for any culture, religion can also be an unwitting sanctifier of racism. In saying this, I am not speaking of the few aberrant white supremacist cults that are obvious propagandists for racism. I am speaking of the local parish, the house of worship on the corner of every cultural neighborhood. As disturbing as it may be, we need to consider how our religious institutions function as transmitters of subtle messages that mask racist conversions.

For racism in religion, the medium is the message. In other words, the basic message itself may be the Bible or the Koran, which speaks of mercy, tolerance, and love. But the medium may be something quite different. In all of our cultures there is a growing phenomenon of xenophobic religious life. While the core claim may be of a loving God, the witness to that faith embodies levels of exclusion, judgment, fear, and intolerance that deeply impact the consciousness of the believer. Rather than providing people with a release from their anxiety about living with others in community, the result of religion may be to actually increase that fear.

Intolerant religions create intolerant people. It is that simple but also that subtle. Religion in America is a force to be reckoned with; we question it at our peril. But we must challenge the notion that any faith community has the right to sanctify intolerance in the name of religious freedom. While we certainly cannot prohibit what such a community preaches, we can challenge it. We can hold our religious leadership to account for the ways in which they may twist the message of love to provide a cover for simple bigotry. This becomes especially critical in a time when global religion is increasingly a ground for conflict. The crusades, pogroms, and jihads of the past have returned with a vengeance. None of our cultures are immune to this kind of religious hysteria. As people continue to look for safety in their faith, they will also continue to be easy targets for those who are quick to identify who the "enemy" is. The perception of living in a world of threat and violence leads believers into the trap of thinking that religion is synonymous with a holy form of intolerance. Convinced that they are the "chosen" people, believers in any faith can easily turn on others as the "outcasts."

Religion is the cultural backdoor of racism in America. It does not matter what culture it inhabits. It does not matter what faith it professes. Religion, as an institution, has the ability to spread the kind of judgmentalism, fear, and ignorance that permits the growth of racism. As delicate as it may be to trace these lines of pervasive racism through our own cultural context, and as risky as it may be in light of entrenched religious lobbies that are quick to attack those who challenge their authority, we must insist that no religious practice is out of bounds for our analysis of multicultural racism. No religious leadership is sacrosanct because no religion is immune to racism. It is imperative that we support and maintain the place of faith in all of our cultures as a vital source of reconciliation and anti-racism. But to do that, we must be willing to see that source clearly by always comparing the message of love to the medium of manipulation.

A Modest Proposal

What will writers be saying about racism in America in the next century? Will it still be our original sin, marking us eternally for suffering and failure? Or will it be a rapidly diminishing force in our multicultural global community? I think we have uncovered three clues that give us the answer.

Our ability to reconcile ourselves in our personal, economic, and religious relationships will determine how successful we are in dealing with racism. Therefore, my modest proposal is that we make these three our priorities for reconciliation. Through this generation of the struggle, we must focus on (a) ending sexism, homophobia, and age vulnerability as primary channels for the transmission of racism, (b) ending our capitalist economic system's ability to deny basic human dignity in housing, health, work, and education, and (c) ending the monopoly of intolerant religious perspectives in speaking for communities of faith. Moreover, I propose that we work on these issues cross-culturally, with each culture taking its share of responsibility to do a rigorous self-analysis. We must put our own cultural houses in order so that we can work more honestly and more effectively together. The hope of my proposal, therefore, is that we will find a new and reinvigorated unity in this century. I believe that if we can be dedicated to creating respectful relationships among all of the people in our cultural communities, if we can demand equal access to basic human needs in everyday life, and if we can bring the best of our religious values of tolerance and love to bear in healing our divisions, then we will have a fighting chance to put an end to the racism that has plagued us for generations. In this way, the writers of tomorrow will have a very different story to tell from the one that we have come to know for too long and at too great a cost to us all.

Questions for Discussion

1. Discuss your reflections on Charleston's statement, "No matter how resistant the sin of racism is to reconciliation, it is still not stronger than our capacity to forgive, to trust, and to love." What are signs to you that this statement is true?

2. In his article Charleston discusses the challenges of racism in earlier generations. What do you believe are the specific challenges of racism in our communities today?

3. What connections do you see between racism and other forms of oppression, such as sexism, ageism, and so on?

4. Why is racism a spiritual issue?

5. What would true racial reconciliation look like? How would the church be changed? How would our society be changed? Be as specific as possible. What would our communities look like if the values of cooperation, solidarity, and compassion were primary? What most hinders us from living into this vision?

5 RACISM AND ANTI-RACISM IN CONGREGATIONS

Building Multiracial Communities
Sheryl A. Kujawa-Holbrook

Sheryl A. Kujawa-Holbrook is Academic Dean and the Suzanne Radley Hiatt Professor of Feminist Pastoral Theology and Church History at the Episcopal Divinity School in Cambridge, Massachusetts. She is also the former chair of the Anti-Racism Committee of the Executive Council and the author of numerous books and articles on racial justice, anti-racism, and the church, including *A House of Prayer for All Peoples: Congregations Building Anti-Racist Community* (Bethesda:Alban Institute, 2002).

Dr. Martin Luther King Jr. called eleven o'clock on Sunday mornings the most segregated hour in America. He also believed that churches should play a fundamental role in shaping the morality and changing the prejudices of the nation. While our churches have long been divided by confessional differences, it can be argued that some of the deepest and most painful separations in American congregations have stemmed from the experience of racism. Overall, the development of American congregations has historically mirrored, rather than transformed, the racism of our society. Generally speaking, the experience of genuine multiracial community within congregations is illusive. Racism has prevailed as an organizing principle of religious life throughout our congregations. The problem is not that racism can be confined to a fringe aspect of religious life, one embraced by persons who subscribe to a faith based on hate and who have not grasped the core of scripture, though such people and groups are flagrant in their racism and bigotry and, therefore, fairly easy to disavow. Rather, the racism that is the subject of this book is at the very core of our faith communities. At a time when racism and race relations are of this nation's major concerns, how can congregations—some of the most segregated institutions in North America, but perhaps the only institutions with clear moral authority—be the catalyst for religious and social change? How can congregations actively build multiracial community? How can we incarnate the vision of racial reconciliation and unity?

Not surprisingly, recent studies have suggested that although mainline churches argue for the importance of inclusiveness, there are comparatively very few truly integrated congregations: only 2 to 3 percent on average, and racially mixed congregations account for only 8 percent of all American congregations.[1] These studies suggest that multiracial communities are not organic; that is, without intervention we instinctively build our congregations according to assumptions of racism and racial division, rather than on a vision of justice and reconciliation. Though it can be argued that there are many individuals within congregations who seek racial justice through their personal vocations, and while it is true that individuals can and do make a difference, their impact is short-lived and temporary if not supported by a committed faith community of believers empowered by God's healing presence. More so than secular political movements, economic theory, or social analysis (although all three are essential), congregations can be sources of both change and authentic racial reconciliation on the personal, interpersonal, institutional, and cultural levels of human society.

The development of a beyond-racism church tradition depends upon a multiple strategy approach to change in congregations. The challenge is the furtherance of personal and structural change at the level of individual believers, congregations, judicatories, and daily

expressions of congregational life. To be achieved, the spirit of multiracial community needs to embrace the whole of congregational
life: worship, hospitality, evangelism, spiritual and educational formation for all ages, pastoral care, and community witness. We need to
push beyond seeing anti-racism and racial justice as a "program" to
seeing it as integral to the vocation and mission of the congregation.

This vision of congregational life must encompass moral policy
as well as public policy-making through which the congregation
relates to other religious traditions and to the broader community.
Finally, congregations must develop a theological perspective based
on multiracial community that offers people a sign of hope in an
enduring culture of oppression. As the population within the United
States grows increasingly diverse, the need for a greater awareness
of cultural and racial differences is a challenge facing all people of
faith who will live, work, and pray within a changing context. For
European Americans this challenge includes an understanding of
the power dynamics inherent in "whiteness" and how the resultant
social power affects persons of other races and cultures. For people
of color, this will include an understanding of how internalized
oppression impacts individuals and communities within a church
and society where the dominant culture remains white. Overall, in
order to build multiracial communities, both white people and people of color will be challenged to grow more culturally competent
and aware of how the history of racism in the United States has
impacted our faith communities.

This is a book based in hope. As imperfect as our congregations
may be, I am confident we can bring about the changes necessary to
make the vision of a church without racism a reality. To be sure, rais-
ing issues of racism in many congregations can feel risky; however,
then the question becomes whether or not we believe that our faith
communities are resilient enough to confront the evils of our era. I
believe that congregations are one of the few places in our society
where people of very diverse backgrounds can work together constructively for the good of humankind. This conviction comes from
seeing congregations that have confronted the racism in their midst,
struggled with it, and moved closer to the reality of multiracial community. In facing racism, these congregations have faced death. That

confrontation itself is hope embodied. Ethicist William Stringfellow once wrote that "hope is known only in the midst of coping with death. Any so-called hope is delusory and false without or apart from the confrontation with the power of death.... Resistance to death *is* the only way to live humanly in the midst of the Fall."[2]

The focus of the essays in this book is on race and racism and its impact from the perspective of faith communities. This focus is not in any way intended to minimize other forms of oppression. Certainly, sexism, classism, homphobia, ageism, ableism, and other "isms" also impact congregational life. Indeed, because of the "interlocking" nature of oppressions, it is impossible to fully address one form of oppression and not another. None of us is free until all God's people are free. In other words, in order to fully examine our racism, we must also examine sexism, classism, and so on. However, it is crucial for communities of faith to recognize the persistence of racism in predominately white religious institutions. It is quite possible to find many predominately white congregations who would describe themselves as "progressive," who might also see themselves as "justice-centered," but who have done little or nothing to address their own racism, particularly on a structural level. In fact, in many of these cases such congregations would deem themselves as ministering in particular with one or several groups of marginalized persons. Racism is embedded in the history of the United States from the colonial era, and the process of maintaining it remains in place to the present day. Though the demographic reality of the United States has changed, the historical legacy of racism remains.[3]

This book is also predicated on the belief that racism is a profoundly *spiritual* concern and central to the proclamation of the gospel. Racism robs us of our wholeness as the body of Christ. Though churches often refer to the need for racial reconciliation today, authentic multiracial community can only be built on a foundation that recognizes the impact of centuries of racism and discrimination on people of color, and the relative and unequal impact of this legacy on white people.

As people of faith, part of the task before us is to learn to look at the reality of racism and other forms of oppression with "gospel eyes."[4] The gospel of Jesus Christ is the story of the liberation of all people. Inherent in this view is the assertion that the church is intended to be a vehicle for human freedom, rather than an instrument of oppression. One of the most frequently heard forms of resistance to building multiracial community are comments that reduce anti-racism training and racial justice efforts to "social issues" or exercises in "political correctness." Turning to our communities with "gospel eyes," however, demands nothing less than re-envisioning our common life through the eyes of Jesus Christ.

Some of the questions that need to be asked in this regard include: What is the connection between my attitudes and behaviors that perpetuates racism? Who are members of this congregation and who are not? What are we prepared to give up to make multiracial community a reality? What are the obstacles to our vision of multiracial community? How are the ways we hold on to a racist vision of our congregation sinful? Though often resisted as a "negative" term, *anti-racism*, when looked at from the perspective of "gospel eyes," is indeed a positive term. In this context, *anti-racism* becomes an intentional turning away from a racist vision of community to a vision of multiracial community where one group is not dominant over another.

Integral to building anti-racism is both learning and *unlearning* how our histories are both a source of freedom and oppression to others and ourselves. The truth sets us free. One of the roots of prophetic action is history. Knowing and coming to terms with our own history, the history of our congregations and denominations, is vital for those who purport to lead the church into the future. "History has its flexible side," says African-American author Toni Morrison. "And each time we critique and examine it, we can deliver other information and insight that in fact changes what we already know about it." Morrison further asserts: "My point is that you are not bound by the future, and, more important, you are not bound by the past. The past can be more liberating than the future if you are willing to identify its evasions, its distortions, its lies, and unleash its secrets and truths."[5]

In "Letter from Birmingham City Jail," Dr. Martin Luther King Jr. refers back to the earliest Christians as a source for prophetic action:

There was a time when the church was very powerful. It was during that period when the early Christians rejoiced when they were deemed worthy to suffer for what they believed. In those days the church was not merely a thermometer that recorded the ideas and principles of popular opinion; it was a thermostat that recorded the mores of society. . . . Things are different now. The contemporary church is often a weak, ineffectual voice with an uncertain sound. It is so often the arch-supporter of the status quo. Far from being disturbed by the presence of the church, the power structure of the average community is often consoled by the church's silent and often vocal sanction of things as they are. But the judgment of God is upon the church as never before. If the church of today does not recapture the sacrificial spirit of the early church, it will lose its authentic ring, forfeit the loyalty of millions, and be dismissed as an irrelevant social club with no meaning for the twentieth century.[6]

It has been forty years since Dr. King's message, yet his challenge to the twenty-first-century church is unmistakable and his vision remains unlived. How can we as faithful people free the church, in a sense, from a history of racism and complicity to more fully capture the values of the earliest Christians? How do the identities, beliefs, ideas, and actions of persons living in the past support or resist a vision of multiracial community? As a faith community, how has God spoken to us, formed us, challenged us, nurtured us, and allowed us to change over time?

Where Do We Begin?

Developing anti-racist congregations is much more than a "program." In his book *The Color of Faith: Building Community in a Multiracial Society*, Fumitaka Matsuoka offers advice to people of faith compelled to build multiracial communities: "The starting point is not to find ways of uniting people divided by fear and violence, but to recognize, celebrate, and learn from God's gift of one creation embodied in varied cultures, languages, religions and races. It is to restore

moral integrity in the midst of the culture of decay by restoring freedom and dignity to the captives we held."[7]

No two congregations have shared the same history or the same
struggles. Congregations who strive to become anti-racist are not
significant because they have all the answers, but because they have
consciously chosen to engage in the long-term process to build multiracial community. They all are engaged in the call to a life of rich
diversity, yet they continue to question, to struggle, to evaluate this
vision. Though organizational theories differ slightly, most suggest a
five- or six-stage process leading to a fully inclusive multicultural
organization, with full participation and shared power at the final
stage. Application of several schema suggest the following stages of
change leading to multiracial community:[8]

The *exclusive* congregation perpetuates the domination of one
racial group over another. Such congregations intentionally exclude
or segregate racial groups on all institutional levels, including deci-
sion-making, policies, and religious teaching. Leaders of such congregations maintain that either one race is inferior to the other, or that
to challenge the racism of the church would be to hinder the life of
the congregation or jeopardize their own position in it.

The *passive* congregation maintains the privilege of those who
have traditionally held power within the church, with the exception
of a very limited number of people of color, with the right creden-
tials and who do not threaten the established order. The organizational model of this congregation resembles that of a private club.
The fear in this congregation is that it will have to change to accom-
modate persons of other races and cultures if they join. In other
words, the majority culture's history, worship, language, or other cultural forms will be lost if those outside "the club" are allowed in.

The *compliant* congregation values multiculturalism on a symbolic level, yet essentially reflects an assimilation model. That is, the
congregation may welcome persons from various racial backgrounds, and it may even hire a staff member in order to identify
with an incoming racial group. However, most other aspects of the
church's ministry remain the same, and there is often an unconscious assumption that the incoming group should make the effort
to "fit in." This model is essentially conflict avoidant, and though

often nominally anti-racist, has put the burden for change on the marginalized group. One fairly common manifestation of this model is to invite "ethnic" congregations to share a church facility or occasionally participate in joint worship services. Though the invitation is usually expressed to demonstrate a desire for more cross-cultural relationships, it does not necessarily also include an invitation to share in the power and ownership of the church. Another scenario in this category is congregations who claim to be multicultural, but will only address race from the perspective of "racial unity" in the belief that to do otherwise is contentious and divisive. The limitation of this approach is that the racism and prejudice of the members are not addressed, but are suppressed for the sake of an artificial "unity" that only exists when the congregation is gathered.

An *anti-racist* congregation is one that has grown in its understanding of white privilege and of racism as a barrier to multiracial community. Such churches benefit from specific anti-racism training at all levels of the congregation, and have developed an increasing commitment to eliminate racism in the congregation. At the same time such congregations begin to develop relationships with communities of color, as well as increasing sensitivity to the affects of other forms of oppression. An anti-racist congregation can envision an alternative multiracial community, but its institutional structures continue to maintain white privilege and white culture.

A *redefining* congregation makes intentional choices to rebuild its congregational life according to anti-racist analysis and identity. By this stage congregations are prepared to recognize and acknowledge: (1) that racism is inherent in all institutions, (2) that racism is instrumental in both historic and current institutional contexts, (3) the need for a commitment to change, (4) the need to put mechanisms in place to facilitate change, and (5) that action is a necessary step in the change process. Congregations engaged at this stage of the change process understand that the purpose of anti-racism education and training is not only to enhance individual awareness, but also to enable multiracial community. In these congregations, members acquire the pastoral support and challenge they need, while at the same time keeping the focus appropriately on sustainable community action. This type of congregation seeks to address issues and

differences so they can be processed in a healthy manner. Congregations at this stage of development undertake regular "audits" of all
aspects of institutional life in order to ensure full participation of
people of color. Here the congregation has transformed their means
of organizing structures, policies, and practices in order to distribute
power among all of the diverse groups in the congregation. Further,
through their commitment to anti-racist action, such congregations
are intentionally accountable to communities of color and work to
dismantle racism in their wider community.

A *transformed* congregation upholds a *future* vision of a new
reality where racial oppression no longer sets limits on human
growth or potential. A transformed congregation is a fully multicultural organization that has overcome systemic racism and all other
forms of oppression. A congregation within this context would
reflect the contributions and interests of diverse racial and cultural
groups in its mission, ministries, and institutional structures. Here
people of color are full participants in the congregation. Moreover,
the boundary between the wider community and the congregation
is porous; the congregation works to form alliances and networks in
support of efforts to eliminate social oppression and to educate others to do the same.

Though each transformed congregation exists in its own context and has a different approach to building multiracial community,
they share several common elements that are supportive for those
interested in introducing cultural competence and anti-racism in
communities of faith. Transformed congregations

- build on an analysis of power and privilege
- continually tie together action and reflection
- create a place for the healthy expression of feelings
- reserve time for cultural sharing and discovery (discourage
  discussion that suggests polarities, e.g., "good people and bad
  people")
- encourage the study of history
- show how oppression harms everyone
- resist attempts to define one objective reality
- be gentle but firm in the face of resistance

• make connections between a vision of multiracial community, congregational life, and the practice of faith.

Congregations are rooted in their local context, and thus it is not possible to suggest a "recipe" for building anti-racist congregations. Multiracial community can be found in congregations of all sizes and all economic levels; what is critical is that the congregation sees anti-racism as integral to the work of the church and in its own self-interest. Each congregation has the potential for transformation through the process of building multiracial community, yet each also will have its own successes and failures along the way, and each will have different challenges to face in the future. Though congregations often grow numerically as a result of anti-racism efforts, each has also experienced the loss of members due to the changes and conflicts that ensued. In a related manner, it is also clear that for such congregations "growth" means more than increased members. To be sure, such congregations have experienced some numerical growth, but in some cases the increase in membership is modest compared to the spiritual growth gained, or the growth in community involvement shared by the congregation, or even the growth in relationships between members. Congregational growth is not exclusively limited to numbers; spiritual growth, growth in commitment, growth in community involvement, and growth in relationships are also important "growth" factors.

Without ignoring the distinctiveness of each congregation, it is possible to suggest that some of the characteristics of healthy anti-racist congregations are also applicable for other contexts.

1. Build on Health. Overall, congregations that build anti-racist communities are those that strive on all levels to affirm the dignity of every human person and sustain relationships based in mutuality and respect. Although all congregations experience transitions, those that seek to build multiracial congregations should do so from the perspective of congregational health.

Though *health* is a relative term, it is clear that a congregation that is already riddled by unresolved conflicts, lacks coherent leadership, is plagued by mismanagement, fails to provide pastoral care to its members, or is avoidant or hostile to the surrounding community will not be in a good position to build healthy community across racial, ethnic, and cultural differences. Though congregations are always in process, health in this respect denotes a community where people interact with each other in respectful and appropriate ways, where feelings and ideas are expressed directly and openly, where the gifts of all are welcomed and utilized appropriately, where clergy and laity use power justly and constructively for the common good and recognize the abuse of power, where there is an openness to ongoing education and issues in the community, and where the spiritual concerns and pastoral care of the members are, for the most part, addressed. In situations where leaders of the congregation were without pastoral care for some time, clergy leaders might decide to spend time assuring members of the congregation that their pastoral needs would be met before implementing major changes.

  2. Know Their History. The study of history reveals both the heritage and traditions of a given congregation, and leads to further discernment of a church's mission and ministry in the present. Congregations conversant about their congregation's history, not only from the perspective of the dominant culture, but also from the perspective of communities of color, have an advantage when it comes to building anti-racist communities. If a congregation is destined to be something more than a museum, the study of spiritual ancestors living in the past are a means to transform a congregation's sense of where they have been and where they wish to go in the future. Certainly, in terms of building multiracial community, the study of a congregation's history is imperative in order to understand the dynamics of institutions and who is included or excluded in the present. Otherwise, the community is built on the premise, "we want to include more people who are just like us."

  Denial of the negative, and in this case, racist aspects of a congregation's history will not only prevent the formation of authentic community, it will serve to maintain social oppression. Just as it is crucial for individuals engaged in anti-racism work to continue to delve into their own personal history for the sources of racist attitudes and beliefs, it is critical for congregations to undergo a similar process of investigation, interpretation, and, ultimately, of renewal.

Such a study of history unmasks the duality of the "American Dream" of freedom, justice, and liberty for all except those who are not in the dominant cultural group. If the truth is to be told, all congregations, just as all human institutions, share a history of heroism and courage alongside a history of failure and fear.

3. Seek Committed Leadership. Leadership is a key variable for congregations concerned with building multiracial community over the long haul. Clearly, clergy and laity who understand the dynamics of power and oppression and who are committed to change are integral. Such leaders tend to view building multiracial community more in terms of long-term *process* than as *product* or *program*.

Many of the clergy and laity who become part of a multiracial community experience a strong sense of vocation or "call" to either anti-racism, racial justice, or to multiracial community itself. At the most basic level, they experience building anti-racist community as a call from God. They tend to share a sense of long-term and "sacrificial commitment." They strive to "walk the talk knowing the risks." Leaders in anti-racist congregations come from different backgrounds, yet many share common experience in that they express some "turning point" or "conversion" in their lives resulting from a direct and personal encounter across the boundaries of race, ethnicity, and culture. Grounded and nourished spiritually, these leaders have challenged their own racism and resistance to change, and thus they are better equipped to lead a congregation through a similar process.

Such leaders envision leadership as a "partnership" rather than a dictatorship. Moreover, the ministry within the congregations featured here blends the pastoral with the prophetic; pastors in these contexts are acutely aware that pastoral care, in the prophetic sense, relates to individuals as well as whole communities. Moreover, they understand the impact of racism and other forms of oppression on those within their communities from a pastoral perspective.

On the skill level, such leaders are good listeners, knowledgeable about power dynamics, reflective preachers and teachers, effective process facilitators, experienced in community advocacy, skilled with the media, and able to communicate across cultural differences. They are willing to take risks, are open to the possibility of failure, and perhaps most importantly, they are persistent. Because authentic multiracial community is difficult to achieve and sustain, it is crucial that leaders in these congregations are able to withstand criticism and periods of frustration and disillusionment. Obviously, change is personally painful to people in congregations, and any leader seeking multiracial community should be prepared for periods of resistance, conflict, doubt, and disillusionment. Yet, those leaders who find joy in the challenge of working for change tend also to be the type of people who cultivate support systems for themselves, and who can accept care from individuals and from the community.

4. Share a Rich Symbolic Life. Though congregations have different "entry points," those committed to building multiracial community eventually experience change on all levels of the organization: education, worship, governance, pastoral care, outreach, and so on.

Part of the challenge of building multiracial community is adapting the symbolic life of the congregation, in terms of worship, music, education, even architecture, to reflect various cultures. Does the worship and music of the congregation reflect racially and culturally diverse language and content? Is the multiracial character of the congregation upheld through religious education programs for all ages? Are people from different races and cultures welcomed to share in leadership? Does the congregation reserve time for cultural sharing and discovery? Does the community regularly celebrate holidays and heroes of the faith reflective of the racial diversity of the congregation? Does the "sacred space" of the congregation—architecture, seating, windows, art—reflect a multiracial, rather than a homogeneous, reality?

Many congregational leaders adapt to the challenges of making the symbolic life of the church reflective of varying races and cultures as part of the transformational process. For some, it is the challenge of introducing Spanish language hymns or prayers into worship. For others, it is affecting the balance between including symbols, texts, and rituals reflective of other races and cultures, and at the same time avoiding the insensitive appropriation of others' traditions. All have had to re-examine their worship, music, education, and all other aspects of congregational life from the perspective of an anti-racist, multicultural vision.

5. Develop Community and Denominational Relationships.
Theologically, the congregations and leaders committed to anti-racist
congregations are from diverse backgrounds, yet they often share a
vibrant faith that is ecumenical and interfaith in nature.
Though all have a denominational home, these congregations do
not confine their mission within the context of one particular church,
nor do they relate solely to other "like" congregations. Rather, such
congregations seek to reinterpret their mission and ministry within
the context of their local communities and with the aim of building
multiracial community. These congregations have developed skills in
community advocacy and have built alliances across churches and
local agencies.

Further, such congregations often benefit from denominational
support and resources. Not only are such congregations knowledgeable about their denomination's work in anti-racism and racial justice, but each contributes leadership and seeks opportunities to
collaborate with others on these issues within their own denomination and with allied organizations.

6. Implement an Action Plan, Monitor, and Evaluate. All the
congregations who hope to address racism, regardless of size or
resources, must implement some formal action plan designed to
build multiracial community, and continue to monitor their progress
and evaluate how they are doing.

In any successful community-building effort, there should be
clarity of purpose and a clear plan of action. As you gauge your congregation's needs and capacities for multiracial community, and discover what has worked for others engaged in similar efforts, you
will begin to develop the strategies and tactics best suited to your
context. Without ongoing evaluation, discernment, reflection, adjust-
ments, and modifications, any action plan will soon lose its rele-
vance, energy, or direction. As long as injustice remains, so does the
need for goals and strategies, action, and analysis. Clearly, the task of
addressing racism within a congregation is a long-term commitment.

7. Cultivate Spiritual Stamina. God calls all humankind to a life
of rich diversity. Our spirituality reflects the relationships we have

with God, other people, and the world, and are consistent with our racial, ethnic, and cultural heritages. Throughout the New Testament Jesus is frequently found in relationship with and in communication with persons of cultures different from his own. The process of living out multiracial community impacts our hearts, minds, and lives and brings about new attitudes and behaviors about God, ourselves, and our larger society. Choosing to live in multiracial community is countercultural, given the monocultural bias of American culture, and requires a great deal of spiritual stamina. A disciplined life of prayer and reflection rooted in a multiracial community of faith is perhaps the greatest source of support for the challenges faced by those who choose to open up their lives in this way.

Congregations are called to uphold and celebrate the joys and the struggles of their journey toward multiracial community through their corporate worship. A great variety of people can become a community if they heed the Spirit, which constantly calls for us to expand our boundaries. The story of Pentecost suggests that in our various cultural identities and through our linguistic differences we can understand each other. It is ultimately our resistance to the Spirit that divides us as peoples: not race, or ethnicity, or religion, or nationality.

We, as the people of God, are called to respond to a world that is groaning under the weight of injustice and broken relationships. Our differences and our interdependence are intended to be a source of strength and a gift from God. As people of faith, we know that the reign of God will not ultimately be built on separatism or political arguments, but on the transformation of hearts: new life, not just reordered life. As the people of God who believe in justice, forgiveness, and reconciliation, we can resist the temptation to stop at the political, social, or even emotional level of racial awareness. Rather, through building multiracial community, we can bring about the healing and wholeness that the world craves. We are all called to engage in a meaningful way the joys and the challenges of our increasingly diverse world. Our future depends on it.

Questions for Discussion

Congregations interested in looking at the next steps for exploring racism within their community can use the following assessment questions to guide the discussion. For purposes of the discussion, leaders may wish to reflect on the questions individually and then compare and contrast the results in a larger group within their congregation.

1. Does your congregation respect the dignity of all human beings, treat all people with respect, and encourage relationships based on mutuality?

2. Has your congregation investigated its history from the perspective of people of various races and cultures? Who is reflected in the historical discourse and who is not? What has the congregation learned from its history, and how does this learning impact the future?

3. Does the worship of your congregation include a diversity of cultures in language, symbols, music, readings, and content? Is there an openness to work in languages other than English? Are officiants and worship planners respectful and inclusive of other cultures, and do they also avoid appropriating others' traditions out of context? Is racism challenged through sermons and worship?

4. Do people from different racial, ethnic, and cultural groups share their stories during worship and programs in the congregation? Do the religious education programs for all ages—adults, youth, children—include material reflective of and relevant to people of various races and cultures? Does the pastoral care of the congregation blend both the pastoral and the prophetic?

5. Is your congregation genuinely grounded in the local community? Are projects planned with, rather than for, the local community? Are there opportunities for dialogue between members of the congregation and local community leaders? Does the congregation seek new members from the local community through outreach, including notices in targeted media? Does the congregation participate in community celebrations and events related to

racial justice, for instance, Dr. Martin Luther King Jr. Day events, Cinco de Mayo celebrations, Black History Month programs, "Alternative" Thanksgiving celebrations, or Chinese New Year?

6. Does the congregation provide structured opportunities to explore racism for all members? Are those in leadership required to participate in anti-racism training? Does the congregation utilize denominational and community resources and networks in this area? Does the congregation have relationships with organizations for people of color for information, referrals, and support? Does the congregation advocate at the judicatory and denominational level for racial justice for all persons? Are the congregation's leaders in anti-racism well-chosen and is there provision for their continuous training?

7. Is the congregation's commitment to multiracial community evident in all publications, including newsletters, websites, and so on? How is the "scared space" of the congregation reflective of multiracial community?

8. Is the governance structure of the congregation reflective of people of various races and cultures in leadership positions? Do the hiring practices and bylaws of the congregation explicitly state that no one should be denied access due to race, ethnicity, or cultural background? Is the ordained leadership of the congregation diverse racially, ethnic, culturally? Is the congregation's committee membership reflective of all identity groups?

9. Does the congregation regularly monitor and evaluate its anti-racism efforts? Are there clear indications of long-term commitment? Does the congregation use the media to make its commitment to multiracial community and racial justice known?

NOTES

Chapter 1

1. Moses' first wife, Zipporah (Exodus 2:21), is identified as a Midianite, Midian being a territory in the Arabian peninsula and possibly on both sides of the Red Sea. In Numbers 12:1 Miriam and Aaron criticize Moses for marrying a "Cushite." Cush could here refer to part of this same Midianite area, though Cush is also one of the sons of Ham and was a way of referring to the lands once under Egyptian influence, including parts of more central Africa. It also seems odd that Zipporah, if intended, is not mentioned by name here. There is reason, then, for thinking that a black African woman is meant.

2. For further reflection on this and other stories and issues involved with racism and anti-racism in the Bible, see Steven L. McKenzie, *All God's Children: A Biblical Critique of Racism* (Louisville: Westminster John Knox Press, 1997). On biblical and related issues see also Randall C. Bailey, ed., *Yet With a Steady Beat: Contemporary U.S. Afrocentric Biblical Interpretation* (Atlanta: Society of Biblical Literature, 2003); Cain Hope Felder, *Troubling Biblical Waters: Race, Class and Family* (Maryknoll, NY: Orbis Books, 1989); Mark G. Brett, ed., *Ethnicity and the Bible* (Boston/Leiden: Brill Academic Publishers, 2002).

3. See Frederick Houk Borsch, "Jesus and Women Exemplars," in *Outrage and Hope: A Bishop's Reflections in Times of Change and Challenge* (Valley Forge, PA: Trinity Press International, 1996), 116–28.

Chapter 2

1. Christopher L. Webber, *A User's Guide to Morning Prayer and Baptism* (Harrisburg, PA: Morehouse Publishing, 1997), 37.

2. Verna Dozier, ed., *The Calling of the Laity: Verna Dozier's Anthology* (Washington, D.C.: The Alban Institute, 1988), 115.

3. I have in mind my faculty colleague Canon Edward Rodman; see also Deborah Flemister Mullen, "Baptism as Sacrament of Struggle and Rite of Resistance," in *Ending Racism in the Church*, ed. Susan E. Davies and Sister Paul Teresa Hennessee, 66-75 (Cleveland, OH: United Church Press, 1998); and Kenith A. David, *Sacrament and Struggle* (Geneva: WCC Publications, 1994).

4. Verna J. Dozier, *The Dream of God: A Call to Return* (Cambridge, MA: Cowley Publications, 1991), 142.

5. Andy Couch, "Life after Postmodernity," in Leonard Sweet, ed., *The Church in Emerging Culture: Five Perspectives* (Grand Rapids, MI: Zondervan, 2003), 81.

Chapter 3

1. See https://implicit.harvard.edu. To understand the results go to https://implicit.harcard.edu/implicit/demo/faqs.html.

2. Shankar Vedantam, "See No Bias," *The Washington Post Magazine*, January 23, 2005.

3. James Weldon Johnson, *God's Trombones: Seven Negro Sermons in Verse* (New York: Viking Press, 1927), 17.

4. Desmond Tutu, "Some African Insights into the Old Testament," in *Relevant Theology for Africa: Report on a Consultation of the Missiological Institute at Lutheran Theological College, Mapumulo, Natal, September 12-21, 1972*, ed. Hans-Jurgen Becken (Durban: Lutheran Publishing House, 1973), 40.

5. Teilhard De Chardin, *The Divine Milieu*, trans. B. Wall, et al. (New York: Harper, 1960), 66.

6. Avery Dulles, quoted in Deane Ferm, *Contemporary American Theologies, II* (New York: Wipf & Stock, 2004), 331. See also Dulles's privileging of the sacramental model on page 334.

7. Vedantam, "See No Bias."

8. Johnson, *God's Trombones*, 19-20.

9. Vedantam, "See No Bias."

10. Ibid.

Chapter 5

1. For a synopsis of recent studies, see John Dart, "Hues in the Pews: Racially Mixed Churches An Illusive Goal," *Christian Century* (February 28, 2000), 6-8.

2. William Stringfellow, *An Ethic for Christians and Other Aliens in a Strange Land* (Waco, TX: Word Books), 138.

3. "Race as a Target Variable" (Arlington, MA: VISIONS, Inc., n.d.).

4. The phrase "gospel eyes" is used by several persons; I first heard it in a sermon by the Right Reverend Steven Charleston at the Episcopal Divinity School.

5. Toni Morrison, Commencement Address (Duke University, Durham, NC, 1992).

6. Martin Luther King Jr., "Letter from Birmingham City Jail," in *My Soul Looks Back, 'Less I Forget* (1963; New York: Harper Collins, 1991), 213.

7. Fumitaka Matsuoka, *The Color of Faith: Building Community in a Multiracial Society* (Cleveland: United Church Press, 1998), 104.

8. Sheryl A. Kujawa-Holbrook, *A House of Prayer for All Peoples* (Bethesda, MD: Alban Institute, 2002), 20-22.

ADDITIONAL RESOURCES

Episcopal Church Center

Those interested in additional resources, including videos, DVDs, books, and articles used in the Anti-Racism Program of the Episcopal Church, should contact the Social Justice Ministries Office of the Episcopal Church Center, 815 Second Avenue, New York, New York 10017 (phone: 800/334-7626, website: www.episcopalchurch.org). The Social Justice Ministries Office can recommend resources suited to your congregation or diocese, as well as provide information on training and program opportunities throughout the Episcopal Church.

Books and Articles

America's Original Sin: A Study Guide on White Racism. Washington, D.C.: Sojourners Resource Center, 1992.

Anderson, Owanah. *400 Years: Anglican/Episcopal Mission among American Indians.* Cincinnati: Forward Movement, 1997.

Angrosino, Michael. *Talking About Cultural Diversity in Your Church.* Walnut Creek: Rowan & Littlefield, 2001.

Barndt, Joseph. *Dismantling Racism: The Continuing Challenge to White America.* Minneapolis: Augsburg Fortress, 1991.

Bell, Derrick. *Faces at the Bottom of the Well.* New York: Basic Books, 1992.

Branding, Ronice. *Fulfilling the Dream: Confronting the Challenge of Racism.* St. Louis: Chalice Press, 1998.

Brodkin, Karen. *How Jesus Became White Folks and What that Says About Race in America.* New Brunswick, NJ: Rutgers University Press, 1994.

Brown, Dee. *Bury My Heart at Wounded Knee: An Indian History of the American West.* New York: Holt, Rinehart & Winston, 1971.

Davies, S., and P. T. Hennessee, eds. *Ending Racism in the Church.* Cleveland: United Church Press, 1998.

DeYoung, Curtiss Paul, et al. *United by Faith: The Multiracial Congregation as an Answer to the Problem of Race.* New York: Oxford University Press, 2003.

Elizondo, Virgilio. *The Future Is Mestizo: Life Where Cultures Meet.* Boulder: University of Colorado Press, 2000.

Felder, Cain Hope, ed. "Race, Racism, and the Biblical Narratives." In *Stony the Road We Trod: African American Biblical Interpretation*, 127–45. Minneapolis: Fortress, 1991.

Frankenberg, Ruth. *White Women, Race Matters: The Social Construction of Whiteness.* Minneapolis: University of Minnesota Press, 1993.

Haney-Lopez, Ian. *White by Law: The Legal Construction of Race.* New York: University Press, 1996.

Hitchcock, Jeff. *Lifting the White Veil: An Exploration of White American Culture in a Multiracial Context.* New Jersey: Douglass Books, 2002.

Jarrett, Emmett, ed. *To Heal the Sin-Sick Soul.* New York: The Episcopal Urban Caucus, 1996.

Kujawa-Holbrook, Sheryl A. *A House of Prayer for All Peoples: Congregations Building Multiracial Community.* Bethesda, MD: Alban Institute, 2002.

Law, Eric. *Inclusion: Making Room for Grace.* St. Louis: Chalice Press, 2000.

———. *The Wolf Shall Dwell with the Lamb: A Spirituality for Leadership in a Multicultural Community.* St. Louis: Chalice Press, 1993.

Lo, Jim. *Intentional Diversity: Creating Cross-Cultural Relation-ships in Your Church.* Indianapolis: Wesleyan Publishing, 2002.

Matsuoka, Fumitaka. *The Color of Faith.* Cleveland: United Church Press, 1998.

Takaki, Ron. *Strangers From a Different Shore.* New York: Little Brown and Co., 1989.

———. *A Different Warrior: A History of Multicultural America.* Boston: Little, Brown and Company, 1993.

Tatum, Beverly Danniel. *"Why Are All the Black Kids Sitting Together in the Cafeteria?" and Other Conversations About Race.* New York: Basic Books, 1997.

Thandeka. *Learning to Be White: Money, Race and God in Amer-ica.* New York: Continuum, 2001.

Thompson, Becky, and Tyagi Sangeeta, eds. *Names We Call Home: Autobiography on Racial Identity.* New York: Routledge, 1996.

Thurman, Howard. *Jesus and the Disinherited.* Richmond, IN: Friends United Press, 1981.

Wu, Frank H. *Yellow: Race in America Beyond Black and White.* New York: Basic Books, 2000.

Websites

AntiRacismNet (www.antiracismnet.org)

Artists Against Racism (http://web.idirect.com/~aar/resources.html)

Beyond Racism (www.beyondracism.org)

The Center for the Study of White American Culture: (http://www.euroamerican.org/links/ar.asp)

The Damascus Road Anti-Racism Process (http://www.mcc.org/damascusroad/index.html)

Mennonite Central Committee (www.mcc.org).

People's Institute (http://www.thepeoplesinstitute.org/)

Project Change (www.projectchange.org)

RaceMatters.org (www.racematters.org)

Recovering Racists Network (RRN) (www.rrnet.org)

Tolerance.org (www.tolerance.org)

YWCA Anti-Racism and Race Relations Programs and Services (http://ywcacolumbus.org/arrpintro.htm)